Praise fo

Girls with S

"Women, take up your swords! This book will give you new strength as you prepare to fight your battles armed with the truth of God. Get ready to be challenged and inspired by *Girls with Swords*."

—CRAIG and AMY GROESCHEL, pastors of LifeChurch.tv, Edmond, OK

"Lisa Bevere is one of God's most powerful voices for this time in our history. Her heart is for the King and his kingdom and to teach God's daughters how to rise up and live out our destiny."

—SHEILA WALSH, author of *God Loves Broken People* and core speaker for Women of Faith

"Lisa Bevere has inspired women all over the globe with her passion to serve Christ and fight to expand his kingdom. In *Girls with Swords* you will be challenged to join the ranks of Christians who are already moving forward in their faith. Don't be taken out of the fight! Stand firm and experience spiritual victory."

—PASTOR STEVEN and HOLLY FURTICK, Elevation Church, Charlotte, NC

"*Girls with Swords* is a prophetic declaration for our time, calling God's daughters to skillfully wield the sword of his Word. Lisa Bevere has a God mandate to unveil our strength in bringing healing, righteousness, and restoration to our world. Read this book with fair warning: you are about to engage in a powerfully courageous life!"

—CHRISTINE CAINE, author of *Undaunted* and cofounder of the A21 Campaign

"*Girls with Swords* is prophetic, biblical, instructive, insightful, and challenging! This is no sweet, girly pep talk; this is powerful stuff for both women and men. We're excited about this book and the potential impact for the church around the globe."

—JUDAH and CHELSEA SMITH, pastors of the City Church, Kirkland, WA

"As you read *Girls with Swords,* you'll be empowered to face your challenges with boldness and learn to live like a hero."

—ROBERT and DEBBIE MORRIS, pastors of Gateway Church, Dallas/Fort Worth, TX, and coauthors of *The Blessed Marriage*

"We are living at an amazing time in history; there is so much pain, suffering, and heartbreak on the planet today—and at the same time such a great opportunity to bring change and be a part of the solution. In her own unique style, Lisa Bevere encourages the King's daughters to understand that we are part of an epic battle and that we need to be prepared. This is not the time to draw back! Read *Girls with Swords* and join the growing company of women who are rising strong on the earth!"

—HOLLY WAGNER, founder of GodChicks and author of *WarriorChicks*

"In *Girls with Swords,* Lisa Bevere once again draws out the hero within and encourages us to become all God has created us to be. Her zeal to see the church united and wielding the Word of God is inspiring and alive. No matter where you are in life, this message will empower you to 're-forge your sword' and bravely face daily battles with courage and truth."

—STOVALL and KERRI WEEMS, pastors of Celebration Church, Jacksonville, FL

"Our friend Lisa Bevere is an amazing woman, an articulate author, and a powerful advocate for women around the world. Lisa truly understands that women face extraordinary challenges in today's world, but, more importantly, she understands that women hold a special place in God's plan. In *Girls with Swords*, Lisa helps women recognize that God has armed them with his Word and made them to be heroes and that through wisdom, prayer, and the power of Jesus Christ, they can overcome this dangerous world and triumph over every injustice. This is an important book that every woman, regardless of age, nationality, or faith, should read."

—JOEL and VICTORIA OSTEEN, pastors of Lakewood Church, Houston, TX

"'God's word is a God sword.' I love this analogy. Through forging scintillating concepts and analogies in this book, Lisa has managed to excel at spreading enthusiasm for having 'an intuitive awareness of our opponent's next move.'"

—DR. CAROLINE LEAF, cognitive neuroscientist and communication pathologist and author of *Who Switched Off My Brain?*

"With a passionate heart and a sharp mind, Lisa Bevere invites each of us to take up a sword of faith and live courageously in the kingdom of God. Each page of this great new book bears witness to Lisa's powerful teaching ministry and reminds us that the battle ultimately belongs to the Lord."

—BETH and MATT REDMAN, author and worship leader, United Kingdom

"*Girls with Swords* is a brilliant display of Lisa Bevere's God-given ability to encourage and equip women to be restored, retooled, and repositioned to take their place in this epic battle and defeat the enemy who has intentionally targeted women throughout history."

—CHRIS and JOY HILL, pastors of the Potter's House,
  Denver, CO

"We have been privileged to feature Lisa Bevere frequently on our *LIFE Today* telecast. Through years of international ministry—including Asia, where she joined with our missions team to help women victimized by human trafficking—she has become well aware of the battles that can only be won with the sword of God's Word. Her message will help inspire and prepare women, in particular, for spiritual warfare."

—JAMES and BETTY ROBISON, LIFE Outreach International

GIRLS
WITH
SWORDS

HOW TO CARRY YOUR CROSS
LIKE A HERO

LISA BEVERE

FOREWORD BY JOHN BEVERE

WaterBrook
PRESS

GIRLS WITH SWORDS
PUBLISHED BY WATERBROOK PRESS
12265 Oracle Boulevard, Suite 200
Colorado Springs, Colorado 80921

All Scripture quotations, unless otherwise indicated, are taken from The Holy Bible, English Standard Version, copyright © 2001 by Crossway Bibles, a division of Good News Publishers. Used by permission. All rights reserved. Scripture quotations marked (ASV) are taken from the American Standard Version. Scripture quotations marked (KJV) are taken from the King James Version. Scripture quotations marked (MSG) are taken from The Message by Eugene H. Peterson. Copyright © 1993, 1994, 1995, 1996, 2000, 2001, 2002. Used by permission of NavPress Publishing Group. All rights reserved. Scripture quotations marked (NIV) are taken from the Holy Bible, New International Version®, NIV®. Copyright © 1973, 1978, 1984, 2011 by Biblica Inc.™ Used by permission of Zondervan. All rights reserved worldwide. www.zondervan.com. Scripture quotations marked (NKJV) are taken from the New King James Version®. Copyright © 1982 by Thomas Nelson Inc. Used by permission. All rights reserved. Scripture quotations marked (NLT) are taken from the Holy Bible, New Living Translation, copyright © 1996, 2004, 2007. Used by permission of Tyndale House Publishers Inc., Carol Stream, Illinois 60188. All rights reserved.

The "Fencing Facts" are taken from Nick Evangelista, The Inner Game of Fencing: Excellence in Form, Technique, Strategy, and Spirit (Lincolnwood, IL: Masters Press, 2000).

Trade Paperback ISBN: 978-0-307-45782-0
Hardcover ISBN 978-0-307-45781-3
eBook ISBN 978-0-307-45783-7

Copyright © 2013 by Lisa Bevere
Sword illustrations by Allan Nygren

Cover design by Kristopher K. Orr; photography by Mike Heath/Magnus Creative

Published in the United States by WaterBrook Multnomah, an imprint of the Crown Publishing Group, a division of Random House LLC, New York, a Penguin Random House Company.

WATERBROOK and its deer colophon are registered trademarks of Random House LLC.

The Library of Congress cataloged the hardcover edition as follows:
Bevere, Lisa.
    Girls with swords : how to carry your cross like a hero / Lisa Bevere. — First Edition.
        pages cm
    Includes bibliographical references.
    ISBN 978-0-307-45781-3 — ISBN 978-0-307-45783-7 (electronic)
 1. Christian women—Religious life. 2. Spiritual warfare. I. Title.
    BV4527.B4943 2013
    248.8'43—dc23

                                                                        2012044356

Printed in the United States of America
2014—First Trade Paperback Edition

10 9 8 7 6 5 4 3 2 1

SPECIAL SALES
Most WaterBrook Multnomah books are available at special quantity discounts when purchased in bulk by corporations, organizations, and special-interest groups. Custom imprinting or excerpting can also be done to fit special needs. For information, please e-mail SpecialMarkets@WaterBrookMultnomah.com or call 1-800-603-7051.

• • •

To all my sword sisters who are ready to raise their voices
and brandish their crosses.

You are the daughters of a valiant, virtuous Warrior
whose eternal, creative word in your mouth
is a living, invincible sword in your hand.
You have been entrusted with a weapon without rival
in a time like no other.
Wield it with skillful finesse, gracious insight,
and in triumphant love, and strike sure.

"From now on people are my swords."
—Zechariah 9:13 (MSG)

CONTENTS

FOREWORD

It's one thing to own a sword; it's quite another thing to know how to use it.

Every child of God has been entrusted with a sword—the sword of the Spirit. We're warriors commissioned to wield the most powerful weapon in the universe. Our Lord and role model, Jesus Christ, is the Sword of the Spirit made flesh. Two millenniums ago he wielded this sword and changed the world. With this same sword he will one day subdue the nations. But for now he charges each of us: "As the Father has sent Me, I also send you" (John 20:21, NKJV).

There is a generation of daughters (and sons) rising up to show the magnificent power of our King. These warriors will bring change to their world by skillfully wielding the sword they've been entrusted with. God has given my wife, Lisa, a powerful message that will train the daughters (and sons) of God to use what they already possess to bring change to their sphere of influence.

I've had the privilege of being married to this great woman of God for more than thirty years. I've witnessed her transformation from a scared, timid church attendee who hid from confrontation to a valiant and splendid warrior-daughter of our King. It's a real privilege to know and work with such a lady. I learn so much from what God teaches her.

I know that this book will train you to use what you already possess. Don't be someone who merely owns a sword. Be a skillful warrior who brings change to your world.

—John Bevere, best-selling author and speaker

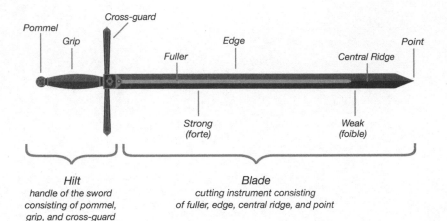

Pommel

Grip

Cross-guard

Fuller

Edge

Central Ridge

Point

Strong
(forte)

Weak
(foible)

Hilt
handle of the sword
consisting of pommel,
grip, and cross-guard

Blade
cutting instrument consisting
of fuller, edge, central ridge, and point

Fencing Terms

Croisé: A parry and riposte made in a single flowing motion. It blocks an attack, diverts it with leverage, and hits without ever letting go of the blade.

En garde: A defensive attitude but also an offensive one. It is, in effect, a position of readiness.

Feint: A bluff that attempts to elicit a response from your opponent by causing him to think you are going to attack when you are not.

Lunge: An offensive movement designed to deliver a hit.

Parry: A defensive deflection of your opponent's blade.

Riposte: A counterattack following a successful parry.

PART ONE

CHOSEN

1

You Are a Target

Christianity is a battle, not a dream.

—Wendell Phillips

In a world already overrun by violence, you may wonder why I would suggest that women of all ages take up arms and join the fight. As you turn these pages, I hope you will discover the many reasons why there is no neutral territory. We do not live *by* the violence of a sword, but the time has come to live *by* the power of one.

The first reason you need a sword is that, whether you realize it or not, you are part of an epic battle, and God does not want his daughters unarmed or caught unaware.

The poignant need for addressing these issues head-on was brought home in an unexpected way. It was early June in the summer of 2010, and I had just returned home from traveling and speaking in five different countries in the short span of four weeks. Mind you, these were not nations clustered together, so traveling meant crossing date lines, exchanging night for day, and bouncing between the Northern and Southern Hemispheres.

Overcome by a persistent strain of jet lag, I was wandering a bit dazed through my second evening home when I realized I was alone with my youngest son, Arden. As I approached him, he patted the sofa and invited me to join him in watching a movie. Thrilled to have a chance to perhaps cuddle with my son, I settled myself in as close as possible and asked, "What are we watching?"

"*The Terminator,*" he answered.

Okay, before you react, stay with me. I am not endorsing the movie, nor am I suggesting that you watch it. I saw an edited TV version, and even then it was eighties awful! But amid the ridiculous hair, disjointed music, and bad acting, I found something valuable I want to share here, because it perfectly sets up the *why* behind the journey of this book.

In case you're not familiar with *The Terminator,* allow me to paint a vastly shortened version of the movie for you. It is the story of Sarah Connor, a moped-riding waitress who is living a boring, mundane life in the hope that one day love will find her. Every twenty-four hours plays out pretty much the same. By day she serves pie and coffee; by night she hopes that one of her blind dates will turn into Prince Charming. By day she works, and by night she waits.

This predictable 1980s pattern is radically interrupted when a robotic assassin from her future shows up. Our hero, Sarah, first learns she might be at risk when she is taking a break at work and realizes a number of women who share her first and last name have turned up dead.

Apparently the terminator, a.k.a. Arnold Schwarzenegger—actor, former governor of California, and ex-husband of Maria Shriver—has time traveled, and anyone bearing the name Sarah Connor is his target. There seems to be no way this cyborg assassin can possibly fail. Not only does he possess the strength and processing capabilities of a robot, but he also is loaded down with the latest in automatic weapons. In addition to all this technology, he has in his possession what would have been the height of eighties data, a sheet torn from the white pages, which supplies him with the phone numbers and addresses of all the Sarah Connors who reside in his target area. As the futuristic terminator systematically works his way down the list of Sarahs, our heroine becomes a bit concerned.

After work she returns to the apartment she shares with a friend only to learn via an answering machine that yet another blind date has canceled, so Sarah heads out to a club. That way, if the threat is real, she will be able to hide in a crowd. It isn't long until the terminator is on her trail, and after a brief visit to her apartment, Arnold shows up at the club with guns blazing and begins wreaking mayhem. Chaos, bloodshed, and screaming displace bad dance moves as everyone scrambles to escape. But wait, there is yet another player in this dark drama.

You see, at the same time that her assassin from the future shows up, her protector from the future makes his presence known while extending to Sarah this compelling invitation: "Come with me if you want to live."

With the choice so obvious, it doesn't take Sarah long to decide: she wants to live. Sarah runs from the bar and jumps in a car with a total stranger, and the two of them try to escape. But the terminator assassin is relentless. A high-speed chase ensues. Bullets shatter the car windows and frazzle Sarah's nerves. No matter where they go or what they do, they just can't seem to shake her futuristic assailant.

This mild-mannered waitress and wannabe girlfriend has no idea why this epic battle rages around her. As bullets fly and cars crash, her protector begins to tell her *who she is.* He explains that in the future she is a legend and that an entire army wages war equipped with the foresight and strategies she recorded and passed on to her son. In the future she is part of a heroic fight against the enemy of all humanity.

Sarah just can't buy that she is a player in this absurd story and is confident there has been a case of mistaken identity. There is no reason for her to be viewed as a threat in the present or the future! In an attempt to bring clarity and some sanity, Sarah counters the claim of her protector from the future. She isn't a hero...she is just a waitress! She doesn't even

have a boyfriend, so certainly there's no son! This nightmare is all a grave
mistake; she's been confused with someone else!

But her guardian insists that she is, in fact, Sarah Connor the hero
and that his mission is to equip and protect her. Understandably overwhelmed and suddenly undone, Sarah yells out, "I didn't do anything!"

To which her guardian counters, "No, but you will!"

At that moment, sitting with my son on the couch, I was arrested.
This line from decades past, "No, but you will!" crashed into my present
with the realization that our enemy often knows who we are before we
discover who we are. And it is high time we each realize the two things
Sarah learned that night. Lovely One,

1. You are a target.

2. You might be a hero.

I say *might be* because the choice is ultimately yours.

A Target

First let's address the idea of you as a target.

If you are a Christian, you are the target of Satan, the enemy of our
souls and the Prince of Darkness. There's no choice about this standing.
There is a very real, highly structured force of darkness in this earth that
wrestles against all who represent God's light and life.

So it is important you know what it means to be a target.

Words that express the meaning of *target* in this context include *aim,
goal, objective, focus, end,* and *intention.*

Satan has made it his aim to distract you from *who you really are* and
what the purpose of your life truly is. It is his focused objective to lure you
off the path of strength, life, and authority and onto a course of intentional destruction.

To move forward with this idea of being a hero, I need you to grasp a new and perhaps somewhat foreign perspective, one that is far more serious than a story line from a movie. For truly a dark and murderous enemy has already realized who you are. He knows your potential and is systematically trying to undermine your future. I believe that *the attacks on your life have much more to do with who you might be in the future than who you have been in the past.*

You see, like the assassin from the future in *The Terminator,* the enemy has your name. Don't let this frighten you. Take a deep breath and realize you are alive with purpose. Don't get paranoid or take this profiling personally, because it is not. The attack is against one and all. For the enemy of our souls, it is not personal; it is just good business.

No one launches a large-scale, systematic assault against something that's not considered a threat. Your name is the same as mine: Christian. This designation is more than an assignment to a religious group; it means "anointed one." You are a beloved, royal daughter of the Most High God. The enemy's approach may look different with each of us, but he will do all that is within his power to hinder or bend your growth to his purposes and distract you from your heavenly destiny. There are no isolated and insulated daughters who can completely escape his attacks. And don't imagine that your current age or your financial or marital status exempts you.

This is not about you. This is not about me. And to be quite honest, it is not even our battle. This battle belongs to the Lord. We are his weapons of light in a world of darkness.

> *The whole course of human history may depend on a change of heart in one solitary and even humble individual.... For it is in the solitary mind and soul of the individual that the battle between good and evil is waged and ultimately won or lost.*
>
> —M. Scott Peck

Women as Warriors

The fact that you are a female makes you a more specific target and the worthy recipient of Satan's enmity.

> I will put enmity between you and the woman,
>   and between your offspring and her offspring. (Genesis 3:15)

Enmity is deep-rooted hatred and irreconcilable hostility. This describes a breach so profound that with each passing generation, Satan's hostility and hatred deepen as he runs out of time and the urgency increases. Never has his attack against women and children been more wicked, obvious, and widespread.

Undeniable evidence of this is found in the conservative estimate that fifty million women are presently missing from the earth. What do I mean by *missing*? These daughters are gone. Never to be found.

The major reason for their disappearance is the targeted practice of gendercide. Genocide is slaughter of a racial, national, political, or cultural group; gendercide is slaughter based on gender. In her recent book *Unnatural Selection,* author Mara Hvistendahl cites statistics that show this outrage: maybe more than 160 million baby girls in Asia alone never drew breath because their birth was preempted by abortion.[1]

In countries such as China, India, and Pakistan, and the continent of Africa, being a daughter puts your life in danger. It could mean you will be abused, sold, neglected, or the victim of an honor killing.

Lovely One, do not think you are safe just because you do not live in a developing nation. Numbers don't lie. Your birth location just means you will be targeted in a different way. The enemy assassin will come at you from another angle, and I believe he is already working hard to distract you so you will never give birth to God's plan for your life.

I do not share these things to frighten you. I want you to know the weight of your moment in history. As a daughter of this age, you are a target. The hero factor is your choice. If you fail to see this for what it is, you will take these attacks against your gender or faith personally and therefore respond on a personal level. But this is way bigger than any one of us. There is no way you can or should fight this battle on your own. This conflict will require heavenly strategy and support. Even though it begins with our individual response, that alone will never be enough. We have to be individually armed with the eternal and trained to work in the company of others.

As horrible as the numbers are, they only hint of a greater darkness. It is time you lift your eyes and lend your voice to what heaven would want to speak into this void. The story line is set. On one side a relentlessly cruel enemy is perpetually bent on your destruction, and on the other side a magnificent prince of unfailing love is equally determined that you realize all he created you to be. Jesus, our Prince of Heaven, will always love you. His love is never ending and more unrelenting than the enmity of your assassin. The role you choose to play in this battle is what is in question. Will you be an unarmed civilian, victim, prisoner of war, or hero?

As you form your decision, please know this: there is no safe middle ground. It is just a matter of time before you must join one side or the other. It is always better to predetermine your position with decisive intention rather than have it chosen for you by passive default. Remember, God *chose you before he even created the earth.*

> In him we have obtained an inheritance, having been predestined
> according to the purpose of him who works all things according
> to the counsel of his will, so that we who were the first to hope in
> Christ might be to the praise of his glory. In him you also, when

you heard the word of truth, the gospel of your salvation, and
believed in him, were sealed with the promised Holy Spirit, who
is the guarantee of our inheritance until we acquire possession of
it, to the praise of his glory. (Ephesians 1:11–14)

From what I understand, by the end of the story it all becomes pretty
simple. There is hot or cold, strong or weak, engaged or disengaged, soldier or traitor, free or captive, and hero or victim.

I know these choices are very black and white, for they are meant to
echo the urgency of our current position as women. I am not implying
that you are under an immediate threat of gendercide. But I am under-
scoring the desperate need for our constructive, proactive response. This
is not the time for you to remain unaware and unarmed, and thus the
purpose for this book.

As I was writing, I reviewed C. S. Lewis's *The Screwtape Letters,* which
is fictional correspondence between a junior demon and his overseer as
they try to ensnare a young man. The brilliance behind this book is that
it grants a window into the enemy's perspective and how he twists and
perverts truth to get us to turn on God.

In one section the demons are gloating about their ability to distort
the women's role: "All is summed up in the prayer which a young female
human is said to have uttered recently: 'Oh God, make me a normal
twentieth-century girl!' Thanks to our labours, this will mean increasingly, 'Make me a minx, a moron, and a parasite.' "[2]

I want to weep at the prophetic irony of this 1942 publication, for it
truly captures the posture of far too many of the daughters of our time.
As I read this quote, four words stood out: "normal," "minx," "moron,"
and "parasite."

First, let's address the issue of normal. When you were born again,
you left normal behind. This doesn't mean you became weird or abnor-

mal; it just means you were stripped of what is average and common when you were covered in his righteousness. You may live in this earthly time period, but you are ultimately a daughter of eternity.

Next, there is the term *minx,* a largely unfamiliar term in our day that means a seductress or wanton woman. Some synonyms for *minx* are *tramp, whore, bimbo,* and *slut.* Sadly, these very words are woven into our culture's twenty-first-century songs.

The term *moron* was first introduced in the early nineteen hundreds to describe someone with the IQ of an eight- to twelve-year-old. In the context of C. S. Lewis's quote, this would mean a generation of daughters who refuse to grow up and transition from the whims of a girl to the wisdom of a woman.

And, lastly, *parasite* describes a person who lives by the support and advantage of another without giving anything truly useful in return. This is the very antithesis of what a daughter of God should represent! We are to live in support of others and grant opportunity to the disadvantaged and not take advantage of others. But look at the covers of women's magazines that line the checkout areas at our grocery stores. Aging would appear to be a disease, while fleeting youth and blatant immaturity are celebrated. Sexual prowess trumps true intimacy, and we are encouraged to live in flagrant extravagance, grabbing all we can in the process. How far we have fallen.

Normal has not served us well, and it is obvious our enemy knows we were made for something more. Who will we allow to form our prayers? The pressure of our circumstances cannot shape our prayers. Our culture cannot be trusted to give us the right words. Our prayers must be structured by heaven. The Creator of heaven and earth is the architect and author of our lives. It is time for the daughters of this twenty-first century to echo heaven's words. Perhaps the longing within you is larger than you know how to put into words and thus the very reason you need a sword.

I believe that in one way or another you long to be an extraordinary, heroic daughter of the eternal Most High God who behaves virtuously, matures brilliantly, and lives with the intent of enhancing the lives of others.

One of the purposes of this book is to help you construct the type of bold, faith-filled prayers (swords) that will specifically address your moment in history.

Old Tactics

Now is not the time to draw back in fear. It is a time when we must rise up and flourish in love. When I became a Christian, I learned that God actually had a plan for my life. It wasn't merely that I had a new destination in the afterlife. I learned my life mattered now. I had been purchased at great expense, and my life was no longer my own to squander. God wanted me to become all he had created me to be.

> Now is not the time to draw back in fear. It is a time when we must rise up and flourish in love.

Becoming who God created you to be is both your best offense and your best defense against the enemy's strategy. He obviously didn't stop you from drawing breath. It is now time to keep him from stifling the spiritual seed God planted inside you. When the enemy oppresses, it is always because he fears what we might become. Remember, oppressors are shrewd, but more often than not they are also afraid. On some level they fear the very ones they seek to oppress. They fear your strength will put them at risk.

"Come, let us deal shrewdly with them, lest they multiply, and, if war breaks out, they join our enemies and fight against us and

escape from the land." Therefore they set taskmasters over them
to afflict them with heavy burdens. They built for Pharaoh store
cities, Pithom and Raamses. *But the more they were oppressed, the
more they multiplied and the more they spread abroad. And the
Egyptians were in dread of the people of Israel.* (Exodus 1:10–12,
emphasis added)

When Pharaoh's oppressive tactics failed to diminish the strength
of the Israelites, he turned to more decisive measures: gendercide and
infanticide. So these are not new tactics of the enemy; they have a cruel
and ancient history. The Bible records two accounts of infant gendercide.
The first is found in the book of Exodus when the king of Egypt issued
this decree to the Hebrew midwives:

When you serve as midwife to the Hebrew women and see
them on the birthstool, if it is a son, you shall kill him, but if
it is a daughter, she shall live. (1:16)

It is important to note that Pharaoh ordered the death of infant
males right before the time of Moses's birth. Was there a sense that the
time had come for the birth of a hero? Did the enemy fear a potential
uprising? Pharaoh adopted a sweeping, systematic approach to eliminate
the chance of both. However, history shows how this large-scale assault
failed to stop the birth of the male child Moses. In a twist of fate, he was
actually raised in the safety of Pharaoh's house as a son of Egypt.

After Moses discovered who he was and what he was created to do,
God used a wilderness to remake him into the deliverer who led the
Israelites to freedom following three hundred years of Egyptian bond-
age. Although Pharaoh had murdered a generation of sons (an army),

God counteracted by raising up a leader to deliver his people and fiercely fighting on their behalf.

The next time in Scripture that the enemy employed infant male gendercide was at the time of Jesus's birth. When the wise men did not report back to Herod, he ordered that all the Hebrew boys age two and under be killed.

> Then Herod, when he saw that he had been tricked by the wise men, became furious, and he sent and killed all the male children in Bethlehem and in all that region who were two years old or under, according to the time that he had ascertained from the wise men. Then was fulfilled what was spoken by the prophet Jeremiah:
>
> "A voice was heard in Ramah,
>   weeping and loud lamentation,
> Rachel weeping for her children;
>   she refused to be comforted, *because they are no more.*"
>   (Matthew 2:16–18, emphasis added)

What haunting words...*because they are no more.* In these two biblical accounts, enraged earthly kings blatantly slaughtered the infant sons they feared carried the potential of destiny. I believe we are again on the threshold of a release from oppression and captivity, but this time it is the girls, not the boys, who are targeted in his attack against all.

> Then the dragon became furious with the woman and went off to make war on the rest of her offspring, on those who keep the commandments of God and hold to the testimony of Jesus. (Revelation 12:17)

Notice the similarities in the motivations of the frightened earthly kings and Satan, the frightened dragon. Both are afraid of being disempowered, both are furious, and both war against a people and their offspring.

All who have not fallen victim still have a chance to choose the path of a hero. The goal of this book is to see you armed and empowered, because as we grow in strength, our God Most High rises up against the enemy.

2

A Sword Is Born

And each man stands with his face in the light
of his own drawn sword, ready to do what a hero can.

—Elizabeth Barrett Browning

You may wonder, why a sword? For self-defense wouldn't the distance and precision of a gun be better? If this attack from the enemy is so far reaching, how about responding with weapons of mass destruction? Aren't swords a bit archaic?

For many millenniums swords have found their way into history and forever etched their romantic imagery on our minds. Swords, as we know them, were first forged during the Bronze Age, a time period around 3000 BC. The instrument emerged from the common spear and knife as metalworkers began to combine bronze and copper. But this vantage is incomplete because it speaks only of swords born in our age. Swords are actually older than we know how to measure in terms of time.

From the Scriptures we learn that long before the age of humankind, swords were created in the forges of heaven and carried by the mightiest of angels in forms we have not yet seen. The first sword we know of in the Bible was made of flaming fire and rotated on its own accord in the hands of mighty winged cherubim.

He drove out the man, and at the east of the garden of Eden
he placed the cherubim and a flaming sword that turned every
way to guard the way to the tree of life. (Genesis 3:24, emphasis
added)

Imagine it! This guardian sword moved. It was a flaming blockade
that guarded the pathway to the Tree of Life to ensure that the banished
Adam and Eve would never extend their hands and take the fruit of this
tree of Eden.

Then as we move further through biblical history, we find swords in
the hands of individuals and armies for purposes of good and evil. The
last mention in Scripture of the mighty sword is as a finalizing agent of
authority and judgment in the book of Revelation:

From his mouth comes a sharp sword *with which to strike down*
the nations, and he will rule them with a rod of iron. He will
tread the winepress of the fury of the wrath of God the Almighty.
On his robe and on his thigh he has a name written, King of
kings and Lord of lords. (Revelation 19:15–16, emphasis added)

Thus from the genesis of human history to the closing chapter of
time as we know it, the sword is present. You and I journey the earth in
a span of time that is much closer to the triumphant close than the sad
beginning. Our time period is likened to the escalation of a woman's
birth pangs, the intense transitional labor that precedes the actual birth.
In this season we find ourselves needing the companionship of a sword.
We are not angelic guardians, so there is no need to imagine we'd ever use
swords to deny someone else entrance into the garden of God's goodness.
Likewise, we are not to execute the role of judge, as this right is reserved

for our King of kings. Rather, in the hands of God's daughters, swords are weapons of life and light.

The God Sword

I want to share something I discovered while crafting this book. Hidden within the combination of letters that spell "God's word" is a "sword." By keeping the letters constant and only altering the spacing, you discover *God's word* is a *God sword.*

Isn't that awesome? This confirms in an unexpected way what we are told by Paul in the book of Ephesians: "the sword of the Spirit, which is the word of God" (6:17).

Everything we need or will need is hidden in his Word, and we search it out like buried treasure!

While in prayer not long ago, I had an overwhelming sense that far too many of God's daughters in this generation are unarmed. Not only would this mean they are ill equipped and unprepared. It would also mean they are at risk and incredibly vulnerable to deception. In the last days our enemy will intensify his assaults with the double-edged sword of false teachers and brethren coupled with self-deception. The New Testament is filled with warnings against deception and false teachers. The gospel of Matthew and the book of 1 John warn us:

> Many false prophets will arise and lead many astray. (Matthew 24:11)

> Beloved, do not believe every spirit, but test the spirits to see whether they are from God, for many false prophets have gone out into the world. (1 John 4:1)

How do we combat deception? We weigh people's words against the truth of God's Word. As the iron of God's Word sharpens our lives, we will be more in tune with what is truth. Regardless of how much we know, if we do not also do, then we are again in peril.

Be doers of the word, and not hearers only, deceiving yourselves. (James 1:22)

In times of battle, swords should be put to use. One of the ways this happens is by bringing the sword of God's Word into the reality of our lives.

> *The knowledge of what is good without*
> *practicing it, turns frequently to evil.*
> —C. MARTELLI, *FENCING MASTER*

Swordsmanship, or fencing, is best learned *before* the heat of battle. Battles are the proving grounds of what you already have put into practice. Conflict has a way of testing the mettle of what was already tempered in your seasons of preparation.

To further illustrate this, allow me to share another story that captures my awakening to the *why* behind writing this book.

In 2009 I was in between back-to-back conferences in the beautiful nation of New Zealand with a morning to sleep in, and I was quite excited about the prospect. It was already past midnight, so I snuggled into my barricade of pillows and with a contented sigh wrapped myself securely in the blankets and sheets.

Before closing my eyes, I turned the face of the digital clock away from me. No buzzer, wake-up call, or cell-phone alarm would be required. I was going to sleep in! I drew the blackout curtains, inserted my earplugs, and ingested my melatonin sleeping aid. Every measure had been carefully taken to ensure that my road-weary body would not be wakened until I was fully rested.

But, alas, such rest was not to be. Sometime between the dark hours of 3 and 4 a.m., I found myself strangely awake with a three-word phrase resounding in my head:

Reforge the sword.

Seriously? What had I been dreaming? I turned over, checked my earplugs, and nestled deeper into my pillows. But I was not off the hook; the statement was repeated:

Reforge the sword.

I made a trek to the bathroom and then climbed back into bed. Somehow I wrestled my way back into the world of dreams, but it wasn't the same. My sleep was restless and shallow, and within my uneasy slumber someone continually repeated…

Reforge the sword.

I woke up and looked at the clock, which now read a little after 4. I knew I would not be able to sleep until I silenced the refrain in my mind. I closed my eyes and tried to place where I'd heard this phrase before, hoping to figure out why I was hearing it now. Was it a passage from a book I'd recently read or from a scene in some movie? As I allowed my mind to wander the course of those possibilities, I remembered the conversation I'd had with one of my sons while packing for this trip. "Is there anything special you would like me to bring home from New Zealand?" I had asked.

"Mom, I'd like anything related to *The Lord of the Rings*," he'd responded without hesitation.

At the time I was doubtful I would be able to honor that request and pressed him for a bit more detail. He outlined some options, so as soon as I arrived in Auckland, I asked my lovely host how to get my hands on *Lord of the Rings* paraphernalia. She explained that I would have a much

better chance of finding such treasures online or in the States. After that
I hadn't given my son's request much thought. But now, in the middle of
the night, I wondered if the phrase I was hearing, "Reforge the sword,"
might be from the movie *The Return of the King,* which was based on
J. R. R. Tolkien's the Lord of the Rings trilogy.

I got out of bed, switched on the light, and sat down to capture a few
thoughts in the hope that afterward I could go back to sleep. As soon as I
started writing, the thoughts came as fast as my messy handwriting could
capture them. The Spirit of God used a combination of imagery, scriptures, and word phrases to initiate what I am now sharing in this book.

I heard the Spirit whisper that far too many factions of Christ's
body wield only pieces and fragments of his Word and no longer lift his
Word as a whole. The Spirit also said that hardships (economic, natural,
governmental, cultural, and social) will be coming upon the earth with
increased frequency and force. These trials will ultimately serve to unite
his people with cause and purpose. And as God's Word is lifted high in all
its weight and authority, answers to these ensuing issues will be revealed.

As I heard these ideas, in my mind's eye I saw individuals lifting
broken fractions of formerly whole weapons and battle standards. The
hilts of swords were held high, but these were useless without the exten-
sion and cutting power of the blades. Upon platforms, which resembled
altars, lay broken points that would normally have served as the ends of
strong blades that could pierce their targets. Alone and unattached, these
sword pieces were nothing more than scrap metal.

Still other warriors possessed broken sword blades that had no han-
dles. The soldiers could not wield these without injuring or harming
themselves, so they laid them aside. Another group held swords that had
no cross-guards to prevent the warriors' hands from sliding down the
length of the blades upon impact. Joined together, all these parts were
mighty and useful and clearly represented a sword's function and proper

use. Isolated, they were edges without points, metal without power, and blades without momentum.

Because of distance and division, many pieces remained unrecognized; they are only effective when they are unified and whole. While we have wrestled with a portion of our armory, the enemy moves about fully armed. I fear he laughs as we foolishly wield our divided words—or words that divide—when ultimately their power is in their whole.

In seasons of relative peace and ease, perhaps sheer fragments of the gospel can sustain us for a short period. But pieces of the gospel will not be enough to provide the mettle we need to stand in a desperate season—just as a church divided will fall.

All that we require to reassemble these weapons of battle in this season can be found in God's Word. Every piece large and small is already awaiting our unified, living declaration. If it takes a furnace of hardship to bring us to a place of unified prayer so that what was separated can be seamlessly joined together, so be it.

Please don't mistake what I am saying here. I am in no way suggesting we compromise or change the Word. I am urgently admonishing that we study, pray, and declare it in a holistic form and let it have its influence on us. The Word of God is alive, powerful, perfect, and pure.

What I heard and saw was a charge to declare his Holy Word in all the wisdom of its counsel and wonder of its strength. It was an invitation to remake the human language in the image of the divine rather than strip the Word of God of its divinity to make it human.

Satan is not afraid of a disjointed church that wields pieces or fragments of God's mighty Word, but he will tremble in terror at the church that rises up with the sword of his Word reforged and expressed through our lives. As we begin to read and apply all the Word, and not just our favorite passages, then we will truly recognize what has been placed in our hands. The body of Christ will rise united when we use our strengths to hone rather than to attack one another. As the church submits to God's washing and correction, she will remember that swords are used on enemies, not friends.

A Sword Reforged

When I returned home from New Zealand, I reviewed the third movie of the Lord of the Rings series to see if the phrase existed and, if so, what was its context. *The Return of the King* is a long movie, so I will only briefly summarize the story line here.

It is the threshold of an epic battle between good and evil, human and demon, light and dark. The allied armies are gathered in numbers too small to combat the wicked horde arrayed against them. All appears lost for the gathering of the brave. Then the princess Arwen sees a fleeting vision with the light of future promise. She returns to her royal father and entreats him to reforge an ancient sword. These are her words:

> From the ashes a fire shall be woken,
> A light from the shadows shall spring;
> Renewed shall be blade that was broken,
> The crownless again shall be king....
> Reforge the sword.

In a context far greater than the movie, these three words branded my heart with a mandate of epic proportions. In the film these words from Tolkien's poetic stanza were interwoven with vivid imagery, which included a fiery forge, a hammer, and a strong and skillful sword smith. The disjointed fragments were aligned and then merged through the repeated processes of fire, pressure, and water until what was partial became powerful again. The sword was renewed.

The formerly shattered monument to the past had become the shimmering symbol of all that could be! In this renewed blade the victories of the past were linked to the impossibilities of the present, and hope for the future was restored.

How different is this from our present condition? Do we still celebrate the testimony of what has been to the neglect of what might be?

I am overwhelmed when I think of all the symbolism the reforged sword holds for us. The sword entrusted to us is more than ancient; it is eternal. Our sword is not attached to an isolated victory; the Word of our living God has proven itself true time and time again. In the Lord of the Rings, this sword created a new order; our God's sword created the heavens and the earth. Theirs was mined from the ore of Middle-earth; ours was forged in the consuming fires of heaven. It is our time to wield the sword of God's Word to make history rather than to simply mark it!

Unlike King Aragorn, our Lord is far from crownless. The question that arises is, are we under his rule? Are we afraid to imagine what might happen if we grasped the Word of God with both hands and allowed it to be our final authority? What if we stopped working so hard to study the Word and lived it instead? What if we simply declared the Scriptures and allowed the Holy Spirit to interpret them? I believe it is time that the church is known for its skill with swords, and it takes much more finesse to heal with a sword than to injure with one.

> They have healed the wound of my people lightly,
>> saying, "Peace, peace,"
> when there is no peace. (Jeremiah 6:14, 8:11)

Cosmetic surgery or superficial healing accomplishes little when what is needed is a heart transplant. People can't look at our world for long and imagine they see peace when there is no peace. We can have peace and must be ruled by our Prince of Peace, but we cannot speak peace where God has spoken judgment. Here is God's remedy for this condition:

> Thus says the LORD:
> "Stand by the roads, and look,
>   and ask for the ancient paths,
> where the good way is; and walk in it,
>   and find rest for your souls." (Jeremiah 6:16)

There is the mainstream road, and there are the ancient paths. One is heavily traveled because it is broad. The others are less traveled because they are narrow. God's Word has the power to light our way and to clear the debris that has covered the path so we can walk in it. The sword of God's Word will separate earthly motives from heaven's intent.

The sword of God's Word will separate earthly motives from heaven's intent.

After having said all this, it may still seem a bit rash, impractical, or fantastical to propose the use of invisible swords in our twenty-first century. After all, wasn't it Jesus who warned Peter that those who live by the sword will die by it as well? (See Matthew 26:52.) This question needs to be answered before we proceed.

To do this let's return to the Last Supper, when Jesus was surrounded by his disciples. Jesus began to contrast what they had known in the past with their future.

> And he said to them, "When I sent you out with no moneybag
> or knapsack or sandals, did you lack anything?" They said,
> "Nothing." (Luke 22:35)

I can almost see them smiling and nodding as each of them remembered the adventure of going out with nothing but a word from Jesus and having everything they needed supernaturally provided. Then Jesus introduced a new season:

He said to them, "*But now* let the one who has a moneybag take it, and likewise a knapsack. And let the one who has no sword sell his cloak and buy one." (verse 36, emphasis added)

Just so you know I am not making this up, another Bible translation says it this way:

"But now," he said, "take your money and a traveler's bag. And if you don't have a sword, sell your cloak and buy one!" (verse 36, NLT)

Not only did Jesus tell them to take money and a carry-on bag; he told them a sword might be more important than a cloak! The days of Jesus being known as "Good Teacher" were over, for he had been marked an outlaw. These disciples were gathered on the eve of *every prophecy* being fulfilled. After a quick inventory of what they had on hand, they found two swords among the Twelve.

And they said, "Look, Lord, here are two swords." And he said to them, "It is enough." (verse 38)

Jesus then headed out to pray on the Mount of Olives, where he wrestled with life and death and was visited by angels as his disciples slept. Jesus was in the process of rousing them from their slumber—to encourage them to pray—when a crowd led by Judas entered the garden.

I am the first to admit that when I am sleepy I am not the sharpest knife in the drawer, but even wide-awake I'd be confused by what happened next. The disciples woke up, realized what was happening, and grabbed their swords—ready to protect their Lord.

> And when those who were around him saw what would follow, they said, *"Lord, shall we strike with the sword?"* And one of them struck the servant of the high priest and cut off his right ear. But Jesus said, "No more of this!" And he touched his ear and healed him. (verses 49–51, emphasis added)

Why bring a sword if you are not going to use it? My guess is that John asked if he should strike, and Peter just went for it. Luke appears to be covering for Peter here, because we know from John's account that it was definitely Peter who managed to lop off the ear. Then the gospel of Matthew gives us a window to what transpired between Peter and Jesus after this sword outburst.

> Then Jesus said to him, "Put your sword back into its place. For all who take the sword will perish by the sword. Do you think that I cannot appeal to my Father, and he will at once send me more than twelve legions of angels? But how then should the Scriptures be fulfilled, that it must be so?" (Matthew 26:52–54)

This passage has always been an enigma. You have to wonder if Peter wasn't a bit confused by this turn of events as well. He probably assumed that because Jesus had told them to get some swords, now was the time to use them. Be that as it may, we can safely assume these swords were never meant to protect Jesus. I am not even sure they were for the immediate protection of his disciples. After all, who needs security when legions of angels are at your command?

Also Jesus didn't tell Peter to get rid of the sword; he merely told him to return it to its rightful place. This also seems a bit odd to me because he next said, "All who take the sword will perish by the sword." Maybe it's just me, but I would have said, "Fling that blade away; it will kill you!" All these incongruities make me wonder if Jesus was speaking in parables rather than in literal terms.

It appears that Jesus tried to prepare them for this approach in an earlier conversation found in the gospel of John. There Jesus explained why he addressed his disciples differently on the advent of his return to heaven than he did when he walked among them on earth.

> I have said these things to you, that when their hour comes you
> may remember that I told them to you.
>
> I did not say these things to you from the beginning, because
> I was with you. But now I am going to him who sent me. (John
> 16:4–5)

At times you can't hear something until its hour has come. You are deaf to it because you don't want to hear it or you don't need to hear it quite yet. When the time is right, there is the aha moment, and what was formerly confusing becomes crystal clear. Certain things can remain unsaid when you are in the company of one another. But what was obvious when you were together becomes a bit murky when you are apart.

To further clarify the sword confusion, let's look at another passage. As Jesus

Fencing Fact

The best fencing, both offensive and defensive, has a sense of balance and moderation.

was leaving, he promised his disciples, "And behold, I am with you always, to the end of the age" (Matthew 28:20).

This promise had greater meaning for the coming circumstances than it did in that immediate moment. When Jesus was no longer visibly with them, this promise spoke volumes as they journeyed into foreign lands and met tragedy and triumph head-on. Not only did this promise serve to encourage them; it still encourages you and me! The hope of this promise is ours.

It is one thing for me to say to my husband who is sitting across the table from me, "I am with you, babe," and quite another for him to hear my words when time and distance have separated us. One is a statement of the obvious; the other is an assurance of the unseen.

This helps us understand why at times it seems Jesus said things that were contradictory in their application. His instruction—buy a sword—was shortly followed by his correction of Peter for using it. The Mount of Olives on the night he was betrayed was neither the place nor time for swords to be drawn. It was a time of consecration and prayer. If the disciples had remained awake, they would have understood that Jesus was in the process of laying down his life, not trying to defend it.

When swords appear, motives are revealed.

Matthew gives a window to a previous time Jesus spoke of swords.

Do not think that I have come to bring peace to the earth. I have not come to bring peace, but a sword. (10:34)

When swords appear, motives are revealed. They have the ability to scatter us in terror or unite us in courage. For all the Last Supper talk of swords, we have no written history of these disciples ever drawing their swords again to defend themselves or to assault their persecutors, which makes me think Jesus was not talking about self-defense or about taking matters into our own hands in our own strength.

Jesus was first tested alone, in the wilderness, after forty days of fasting and then tested again, surrounded by friends, in a garden, following a feast. But the first trial was not that different from the final one. In the first, Satan encouraged the starving Jesus to turn the stones before him into bread. His request could even have been viewed as scriptural; after all, Moses had provided bread for the children of Israel during their sojourn in the wilderness.

But he [Jesus] answered, "It is written,

" 'Man shall not live by bread alone,
    but by every word that comes from the mouth of God.' "
        (Matthew 4:4)

One miraculous act was about feeding others; the other was about feeding one's self. Later in his earthly ministry, Jesus actually revealed how well he understood this difference when he referred to himself as the bread of life.

Jesus said to them, "I am the bread of life; whoever comes to me shall not hunger, and whoever believes in me shall never thirst." (John 6:35)

Was Jesus speaking in literal terms here? No, I have experienced both physical hunger and thirst since I've encountered Jesus. The fast in the wilderness had changed Jesus from one who lived on bread to one who provided living bread, which is Jesus, the Word made flesh.

Satan also challenged Jesus to demand God's intervention by way of a forced rescue if Jesus would leap off the temple pinnacle.

"If you are the Son of God, throw yourself down, for it is written,

" 'He will command his angels concerning you,'

and

" 'On their hands they will bear you up,
lest you strike your foot against a stone.' ' "

Jesus said to him, "Again it is written, 'You shall not put the Lord your God to the test.' " (Matthew 4:6–7)

Jesus knew he had not come to throw himself down in some foolish attempt to prove to the religious leaders he was God's Son. Instead, he had come to lift us all up on the cross. When Satan tried to tempt Jesus with all the kingdoms of this earth and their glory, Jesus used the sword of the Word again:

"Be gone, Satan! For it is written,

" 'You shall worship the Lord your God
and him only shall you serve.' "

Then the devil left him, and behold, angels came and were ministering to him. (verses 10–11)

Apparently these angels show up after we pass the "it is written" test! Just as Satan did with Jesus, Satan attempts to twist the meaning and therefore the application of God's Word in the hope that we will misuse his promises for self-preservation, the admiration and recognition of others, or selfish gain. As Satan strikes with a distortion of truth, we counter with a declaration of truth.

Throughout the history of sword fighting, there was a common saying whenever a duel was called to settle a question of honor: "The sword is truth."

The hour has come for us to live by the sword of truth, which is the Word of our God. To achieve that end, this book will be sprinkled with images of swords and fencing terminology so we can become more thoroughly acquainted with God's weapon of choice.

The terms *sword fighting* and *fencing* can be used interchangeably. *Fencing* is actually derived from the word *defense,* and we have no greater defense than the Word of God.

In my study of fencing, I learned it was one of the few sports in which women can match men, because fencing requires mental strategy over physical strength. Successful fencing incorporates small, precise moves rather than larger strikes. Matches are won through an intuitive awareness of your opponent's next move rather than overconfidence in your own game.

3

You Might Be a Hero

It is impossible to win the race unless you venture to run,
impossible to win the victory unless you dare to battle.

—Richard M. DeVos

We have addressed why you are a target. Then we discussed why the sword is your weapon of choice. Now let's talk about being a hero.

> A female hero or heroine: superwoman, champion, conqueror, star, protagonist, lead, and brave woman.

Is the realization that you have been targeted simply because you *might* be a hero perhaps a bit daunting? Honestly, who gets excited when they hear they are marked for an attack? But as you know, you are not normal. You're an anointed daughter of the Most High God, the creator of heaven and earth and of all things seen and unseen. This makes you a potential threat to the enemy.

I know you realize the battle is real and the stakes are high, but like our friend Sarah Connor, maybe you haven't done anything *yet*. But deep inside you know that one day you will. And here is the great part: your journey toward becoming a hero begins when you simply grant God permission to have his way.

Recently someone I consider a modern-day hero, who is making a difference worldwide and inspiring thousands, asked me, "Do you think I'm even called to the ministry?"

I laughed out loud! Of course she is. But her question and momentary confusion were sincere. Why? Sometimes the mist of our time clouds our eternal perspective. Never doubt you are part of the story of your day.

> *We can be in our day what the heroes of*
> *faith were in their day—but remember at the*
> *time they didn't know they were heroes.*
> —A. W. TOZER

It stands to reason that if these Bible heroes of faith didn't know that they were heroes in their day, we may likewise be clueless in our day. We are in good company, because, like us, they were heroes unaware.

God Makes Heroes Out of Nobodies

Just as our lives are a gift, the story we are in is also a gift that we open up by faith. We don't have to figure out our hero qualifications and then try out for the role. God has already written us into the story line of faith heroes, and it is an epic of triumphant proportions filled with miracles, battles, signs, and wonders.

> The story we're given is a God-story, not an Abraham-story.
> (Romans 4:2, MSG)

Let's start where our story begins—with the first hero of faith, Abraham, who began his sojourn into history when he stopped trying to sort things out on his own. Like many of us, Abraham was the descendant of an idolater (see Joshua 24:2). Idolatry is based on worshiping what we can construct with our own hands. When God is looking to do something grander than we can design, he brings us into his plans—rather than blessing what we have constructed.

We read in Scripture that

Abraham entered into what God was doing for him, and *that* was the turning point. He trusted God to set him right instead of trying to be right on his own. (Romans 4:3, MSG)

The question before us is, are we ready to do the same? If so, then it is time to step into what God has already done for us. This allows his Spirit to begin that new work within us. This action shows we believe that in him we are more than conquerors. As we turn this corner and set our hearts on this course, he positions us so that something unseen but wildly significant can happen. And when we walk in tandem, we not only gain his perspective; we are granted his authority.

So Jesus said to them, "Truly, truly, I say to you, *the Son can do nothing of his own accord,* but only what he sees the Father doing. For whatever the Father does, that the Son does likewise." (John 5:19, emphasis added)

Accord means "in agreement, unity," and "in harmony with." If Jesus, the only begotten Son of God, did nothing out of sync with his Father, then we, his hero daughters, will accomplish nothing of eternal value if we don't likewise follow his lead!

The Bible describes heroes, like Abraham, who have gone before us as those "willing to live in the risky faith-embrace of God's action for them" (Romans 4:12, MSG). Just as we trust that, in Christ, God eradicated our past, we believe that, in Christ, he is already acting on our behalf in the future. The relationship is further explained in this way:

> We call Abraham "father" not because he got God's attention
> by living like a saint, but because God made something out of
> Abraham when he was a nobody. (Romans 4:17, MSG)

We can't save ourselves by living right. No one is righteous save Jesus, the Son. So we throw ourselves into the mix of what God did through faith for Abraham, and we likewise give God our permission to make *something* out of a *nobody*. That something might look like a courageous action hero formed out of a formerly complacent broken daughter. When we enter into God's actions on our behalf, we become action heroes. Our ancestors distinguished themselves from the masses by their *acts of faith* or *faith actions*. They attained the status of heroic men and women in the history of God.

> The fundamental fact of existence is that this trust in God, this
> faith, is the firm foundation under everything that makes life
> worth living. It's our handle on what we can't see. *The act of faith*
> is what distinguished our ancestors, set them above the crowd.
> (Hebrews 11:1–2, MSG, emphasis added)

Heroes Are People of Substance

We see these faith actions outlined verse by verse in the book of Hebrews where the phrase *by faith* is echoed time and time again. The following list is a sampling of what these heroes accomplished by faith.

- Set the precedent for acceptable sacrifices
- Skipped death

- Pleased God
- Built a massive ark in the middle of dry land
- Drew the line between good and evil
- Traveled to places unknown
- Lived as strangers in the land
- Kept their eyes on the eternal
- Received what God did for them by faith
- Became pregnant in old age and birthed a nation
- In times of testing offered the promise back to God
- Reached into the future and blessed their descendants
- Prophesied destiny and the Exodus
- Braved the king's decree and hid their son
- Refused a privileged royal life with the oppressors and chose hardship among God's people, who were oppressed
- Turned from the angry earthly king to obey the invisible eternal God
- Celebrated the Passover
- Crossed the Red Sea on dry land
- Marched around Jericho seven times
- Welcomed spies and escaped destruction
- Toppled kingdoms
- Made justice work
- Took the promises for themselves
- Were protected from lions, fires, and swords
- Turned disadvantage to advantage
- Won battles
- Routed enemies
- Received their loved ones back from the dead

From this massive list I am going to choose just four things you can receive into your life by faith so you can immediately adopt the attitude of an action hero.

1. **Receive what God has already done for you by faith, and walk it out!** Abraham lived what he had received. He didn't turn back or say, "God has finished this work, so I can stop living by faith as a nomad in tents." He consistently walked in what had been revealed to him throughout the length of his days.

2. **Please God.** Our Father is pleased when his children lay hold of the invisible substance from which he formed their lives and begin to walk in the revelation of who he is to them. Hebrews tells us that "without faith it is impossible to please him, for whoever would draw near to God must believe that he exists and that he rewards those who seek him" (11:6). Living by faith pleases God. In addition to being the "assurance of things hoped for" (11:1), faith is confidence, trust, devotion, constancy, and loyalty. It is a life completely confident and spent in allegiance to our King. The opposite of living by faith would be living a life of disloyalty and disbelief. Choosing the route of pleasing God accomplishes the next objective.

3. **Bless your descendants**. When we intentionally choose life, blessing, and obedience, we position a thousand generations in a similar manner! Listen to what Psalm 105:7–9 promises us: "He is Jehovah our God: His judgments are in all the earth. He hath remembered his covenant for ever, the word which he commanded to a thousand generations, the covenant which he made with Abraham, and his oath unto Isaac" (ASV).

4. Choose to live as a stranger in this land. This means living
with the understanding that we are just passing through this
world. We are rooted in Christ. Our life comes from him;
therefore, we do not allow our roots to go too deep here.
Plants draw water and their nutrients through their root systems. We draw on God and give out to this earth. Living as a
stranger to this earth is not equivalent to acting strange on this
earth. It's all about where you put your focus: "Set your minds
on things that are above, not on things that are on earth. For
you have died, and your life is hidden with Christ in God"
(Colossians 3:2–3).

Heroes Have Attitude

This list of awesome exploits from Hebrews 11 was accomplished by
people who were very much like you and me. The only difference between them and us may be that they had adopted heaven's perspective
and refused to live according to the limits of this earth. We are their
descendants. This is our heritage!

In addition to all that was just listed, they braved the following challenges of hardships. Some were tortured but never gave in. They endured
abuse, whips, dungeons, and chains. Some were stoned, sawed in two, or
murdered, while others wandered the earth in animal skins—homeless,
friendless, and powerless in their day. Yet their lives speak powerfully to
us today. The Bible finishes the description of these heroes by saying,
"of whom the world was not worthy—wandering about in deserts and
mountains, and in dens and caves of the earth" (verse 38).

This stirs my heart. I want to live in a way that makes me more of a
citizen of heaven than of earth! We don't have to be tortured or sawed

in two to have this perspective change. But we may need to change some of our expectations.

Heroes Seize Their Moment

While I was typing these very words, the city where we live caught on fire, and we witnessed firsthand God's deliverance.

I was in our basement on a Wednesday morning, working like a fiend, when my husband, John, came home and told me I needed to return with him to our offices. He and the ministry staff had prayed on Tuesday about the Waldo Canyon fire, and, sadly, that night we watched from our front porch as the fire traveled with the wind down the mountainside and consumed hundreds of houses in its path. Thirty-two thousand people in our city had to be evacuated. So again on Wednesday morning, John and the staff prayed amid threats of a possible evacuation of our offices.

Then the situation worsened. Many of our staff members were understandably afraid as the fire threatened both their homes and livelihood. As leaders we were discussing what we needed to get out of our building when suddenly John got angry. He came to me and said, "Lisa, we are going back to our offices and praying a third time."

You may have to fight a battle
more than once to win it.
—Margaret Thatcher

At first I protested. I had a manuscript to write. Then I realized it was a chance to live what I was studying in Hebrews about heroes, how they…

quenched the power of fire, escaped the edge of the sword, were made strong out of weakness, became mighty in war, put foreign armies to flight. (Hebrews 11:34, emphasis added)

John and I headed to our office, and on the way we called a friend with fierce faith. At times when you are in the midst of a fire, you need someone who is *not* in the fire to help you find your way out of the smoke. We shared in detail what was going on, and John explained what was in his heart and what we were believing for. Her heart leaped right alongside ours in powerful agreement. She reminded us of the memorial stones in our past. You see, this wasn't the first time we had faced the threat of fire, and we needed the reminder of what we had learned *then* as we faced this battle *now.*

Maybe you are thinking, *But I don't have a memorial stone to carry forward.* Well, I have great news for you. All of the exploits listed in Hebrews 11 are raw material for you to build with.

We hung up with our friend and promised to call her back, because she wanted to be part of our prayer time at the office. The three of us were so expectant that we couldn't wait to pray and then watch to see how our Almighty God would answer. We gathered our staff, and John took a marker in hand and began to write out on a whiteboard what we were praying for. We prayed that the fire would spread no farther and would begin to consume itself. This would mean that no more structures would be burned or lives lost and that our current pre-evacuation status would never become mandatory. As I looked around the room at the faces of our staff, I saw fear, faith, concern, questions, and even excitement. Then we all went outside and began to pray.

Fencing Fact

In fencing, if you fall into playing your opponent's game, you are as good as doomed.

Keep in mind that this was the third time our staff had gathered. I sensed that some were a bit "weary in well doing." But as we joined voices and hands and made a circle, the strength of our prayers began to grow as everyone engaged. I don't know how long we prayed, but I do know we all prayed until we saw something in the distance… We saw the answer. Three of us saw God answering by fire…as the fire of heaven consumed the fire on earth. Don't even ask me to make sense of this, because I can't.

As we prayed, we literally felt a low-pressure front move in, and the temperature dropped perceptibly. Less than an hour after John and I left the office, rain fell in our area, and the winds shifted. By evening all the fires that had been visible from our front porch the night before were gone. Not one more home burned to the ground. The news reports said the fire was moving back upon itself.

Now, I know that, in addition to our team, many others were praying. We saw what can happen when we purposefully join our voices in strength and faith with others. Brave firefighters, police, the National Guard, and other branches of the military were working tirelessly to combat the flames. It was time for us to pray as hard as they were working, because if they were willing to stand on the edge of earth's flames, then the least we could do was cry out for heaven's assistance.

In addition to praying, our staff worked hard to connect evacuees with host families. Heroes understand they combine action with prayers!

Heroes Are Part of a Connected Legacy

In Hebrews 11 we read,

Each one of these people of faith died not yet having in hand what was promised, but still believing. How did they do it?

They saw it way off in the distance, waved their greeting, and
accepted the fact that they were transients in this world. (verse
13, MSG)

Just what did those faith heroes of old see in the distance? Was it
expensive houses and cars? I don't think so! You do not wave at or greet
things; you wave at and greet *people*!

If we are to follow their example, we must become farsighted.

These heroes did not look at what was in their hands, because they
were too busy waving to something on the distant horizon. Heroes are
people of assured hope and heaven's conviction, because faith is the substance of things hoped for and the very evidence of things that are yet
unseen (see 11:1, KJV).

Read the following verse, and be at once awed and humbled because
our God Most High has counted you and me worthy to be numbered
as one of them.

And all these, though commended through their faith, did not
receive what was promised, since God had provided something
better for us, that apart from us they should not be made perfect.
(verses 39–40)

We are linked to the long chain made out of their lives. We are part
of the final act in their ongoing story. All of their heroic acts are waiting
to be completed when they are joined together with ours.

As I review the lives of these legends of faith, I don't understand why
we were destined to see up close what they were only able to see as a speck
in the distance. They labored without ever tasting the fruit of the very
fields God is allowing us to harvest.

- They wandered in harsh conditions; we gather in air-conditioned buildings.
- They were homeless; we have found our home in the house of God.
- They sang alone in the wilderness; we lift our voices among thousands.
- Their hands were empty; our hands are full.

What is the faith substance we contribute to this legacy of faith then and now?

It is time we pray that the Lord of the harvest opens our eyes and widens our gaze so that we, too, might see beyond the obvious and live out the actions of heaven's heroes. Could it be that we bring the action to the words they released? That we lay our hands on that which they received only in a figure?

> Therefore, since we are surrounded by so great a cloud of witnesses,
> let us also lay aside every weight, and sin which clings so closely,
> and let us run with endurance the race that is set before us, looking
> to Jesus, the founder and perfecter of our faith, who for the joy that
> was set before him endured the cross, despising the shame, and is
> seated at the right hand of the throne of God. (Hebrews 12:1–2)

We know we were the joy set before Jesus. I often wonder if these heroes of old aren't the very ones who are cheering us on. Are we not surrounded and encompassed by a cloud of witnesses as surely as we are surrounded and encompassed by angel armies?

As the realization grows of how in him we are heroes and he is the hero within, it should overpower any fear we may have felt when we learned we were targets. We need to throw our shoulders back and declare, "I am positioned for overwhelming triumph because I am 'from God and have overcome them, for he who is in [me] is greater than he who is in the world' " (1 John 4:4).

Even now I pray that these words stir the faith that has been seeded within your heart and that the hope of *hero* inspires you. It is exciting to look in the mirror and realize there is far more to you than anyone can actually see. The realm of the unseen holds your secret hero identity. Being a hero is an act of worship.

Heroes Are Superhuman

The godly people in the land
   are my true heroes!
   I take pleasure in them! (Psalm 16:3, NLT)

I love this verse because it equates godliness with heroism. What does it mean to be godly? Some of the words that define godly are *holy, heavenly, transcendent,* and *superhuman.* This means again that we operate

Not by might, nor by power, but by my Spirit, says the LORD of hosts. (Zechariah 4:6)

Our hero status is not dependent on our human might or power or even our human spirit; it comes from the power of his Spirit. Because we are called to be transcendent and superhuman, it's time we acted the part. Life in the Spirit means we no longer give way to the base actions and emotions that tether us to our own strength and striving. Nor can we allow the enemy entrance through our actions.

For while there is jealousy and strife among you, are you not of the flesh and behaving only in a human way? (1 Corinthians 3:3)

Do you hear this? Acting human isn't large enough to steward what is inside of us. We actually behave in a superhuman way when we eliminate jealousy and strife from the equation of our lives. We supersede the fleshly norm by choosing to walk in one accord.

Superheroes are able to help the endangered and frightened because they understand they answer to a higher power. Imagining that any of us can be a hero in our own strength will not take us very far. God is our power source, and we are accountable to the One who empowers us and who has granted us the privilege of sharing his name—Jesus.

Heroes Are Brave

Courage in danger is half the battle.
—Plautus

Heroes are *always brave,* but don't imagine that *always brave* translates to *never afraid.* I have found the following simple insight from Ralph Waldo Emerson to be profoundly true: "A hero is no braver than an ordinary man, but he is braver five minutes longer."

Fencing Fact

To have a say in the matter, to choose your response—this is a real fencer.

There are times when being "braver five minutes longer" actually means being quiet when you are attacked, which allows God to have the final word. At other times "braver five minutes longer" means standing your ground and being constant. Being "braver five minutes longer" is never yielding voice or ground when the defenseless are under attack. Often battles are won, lies are exposed, and enemies are conquered because you are the last one standing on the field. Courage will keep you steadfast.

Life is filled with terrifying moments, and we cannot stop the on-slaught of fear any more than we can hold back the wind. But we can always choose our response. The very winds that cause the eagle to soar later in life terrified it when it was an eaglet. Allow fear to drive you toward God.

Heroes Have Something More to Them

All heroes have—shall we say—something more to them simply because they have attached their lives to something larger.

> *A hero is someone who has given his*
> *or her life to something bigger than oneself.*
> —Joseph Campbell

Heroes tend to champion causes rather than champion themselves. Being motivated by something outside themselves drives them to risk being *more* daring, compassionate, willing, responsible, and courageous. Heroes understand there is always more than meets the eye. Heroes are not afraid to stand up or stand out. This willingness to rise above the realm of normal makes them appear extraordinary.

At the time of this writing, the movie *The Avengers* is among the top three box office hits of all time. It is interesting to note that an avenger is a righter of wrongs. Part of what makes this movie work is that these avengers are unique individual heroes who learn to work as a team. Separate they are mighty; together they prove to be invincible.

Captain America has the winning combination of superior strength and honor, but he's a bit naive. Thor is winsome and good hearted and wields an unconquerable hammer, but he trusts his brother when he shouldn't. Iron Man is brilliant and funny with a reticent character, but he is also sarcastic and a bit jaded. The Hulk has raw brute strength that he has little to no control over. The Black Widow is extremely agile and adept under pressure but carries within her a dark past. And the list could include a plethora of other superheroes, but the point is that all of them have both unique strengths *and* weaknesses.

Other than Jesus, every Bible hero had strengths and weaknesses! Superheroes are found in both genders and come in all shapes and sizes… just as you and I do.

Christian means follower of Christ and anointed one. We worship our hero, Jesus, by allowing God's provision and grace to make us heroes. Listen to Paul's charge to the church of Ephesus:

God is strong, and he wants you strong. So take everything the Master has set out for you, well-made weapons of the best materials. And put them to use so you will be able to stand up to everything the Devil throws your way. This is no afternoon athletic contest that we'll walk away from and forget about in a couple of hours. This is for keeps, a life-or-death fight to the finish against the Devil and all his angels.

Be prepared. You're up against far more than you can handle on your own. Take all the help you can get, every weapon God has issued, so that when it's all over but the shouting you'll still be on your feet. Truth, righteousness, peace, faith, and salvation are more than words. Learn how to apply them. You'll need them throughout your life. God's Word is an *indispensable* weapon. In the same way, prayer is essential in this ongoing warfare. Pray hard and long. Pray for your brothers and sisters. Keep your eyes open. Keep each other's spirits up so that no one falls behind or drops out. (Ephesians 6:10–18, MSG)

There is a massive amount of information in this passage. Let's item-
ize these significant points, because these verses in Ephesians outline the
mandate of this book.

1. God is strong, and he wants his daughters strong!
2. His weapons are supreme.
3. With these weapons in hand, nothing the enemy throws
   at you will knock you off course.
4. You are in a spiritual battle between life and death.
5. If you prepare now, you won't be caught off guard.
6. You can't do this in your own human strength.
7. Truth, righteousness, peace, faith, and salvation are life
   applications!
8. God's Word is an indispensable weapon.
9. Prayer is not optional.

Our Heavenly Father anticipated each and every one of our needs
and has empowered us to overcome. The finest personalized infallible
weaponry awaits us. These timeless elements have the power to win battles that are immediate and also in our future. We are in the midst of a
struggle between light and dark, and life and death hang in the balance.
We must not turn and run in fear.

As long as we walk this earth, the dragon will form weapons that he
hopes will prevail against us. The enemy will rage and
wage war against all God's daughters. But he
will not prevail, because we possess swords
forged in fire. As the daughters of God
draw their swords, the enemy draws back.

Face forward, stand your ground,
lift your sword, and let the enemy see the
lovely face of a hero.

Fencing Fact

Curb your adversary's aggressiveness by attacking every time he comes too near during the preparation of his own offensive.

4

The Battleground

For we do not wrestle against flesh and blood,
but against the rulers, against the authorities,
against the cosmic powers over this
present darkness, against the spiritual forces
of evil in the heavenly places.

—Ephesians 6:12

In this chapter we will answer the questions "Where is the battle?" and "Who is my enemy?"

The quick, simple answers are that our battle is fought in a realm unseen, and our enemies are not the people we know.

We live in an ever-changing world where time as we know it will soon yield to eternity: "For the present form of this world is passing away" (1 Corinthians 7:31).

The earth and all that is within it were created by what we cannot yet see.

Take the mighty atom as an example. Can the naked eye see it? No. But the power and wonder of the atom does not cease to exist because we cannot see it. In *The Screwtape Letters* one demon warned another, "Above all, do not attempt to use science (I mean, the real sciences) as a defence against Christianity. They will positively encourage him to think about realities he can't touch and see."[3]

We cannot assume that just because something is outside our realm of notice it has no influence on us. It is time we use our minds. Here is the bad news: your mind is engaged in a wrestling match, and there is no way for you to opt out.

> For we do not wrestle against flesh and blood, but against the rulers, against the authorities, against the cosmic powers over this present darkness, against the spiritual forces of evil in the heavenly places. (Ephesians 6:12)

The good news is that you have the power to choose what you wrestle with. Our enemy wants to divert our focus from the unseen wrestling match so that we are distracted and controlled by a shadowed expression of evil. He doesn't want to see us strike at the source that is actually casting the shadow. Attempting to defeat the enemy by wrestling with people could be likened to trying to destroy a tree by picking all its fruit. To kill a tree, you must destroy the root system.

There is an entire underground system of darkness in place, which often operates or gains expression through the lives of people. People have not targeted you, even though at times it may feel that way. Something far more cunning and ancient has you in its sights, because the dragon is afraid of what you carry.

Just as surely as labor precedes natural birth, there are temporal battles before eternal dreams. It seems right now a *nightmare* obscures our Lord's most worthwhile and glorious *dream*. Individually, we are his dream, fought for and won. But his hope for us doesn't stop there; we see his dream for all of us reflected in this Spirit-breathed prayer:

I do not ask for these only, but also for *those who will believe in me through their word,* that they may all be one, just as you, Father, are in me, and I in you, that they also may be in us, so that the world may believe that you have sent me. The glory that you have given me I have given to them, that they may be one even as we are one, I in them and you in me, *that they may become perfectly one,* so that the world may know that you sent me and loved them even as you loved me. (John 17:20–23, emphasis added)

At the table of his last supper, surrounded by the eleven believing disciples, Jesus was praying for us. He included us who would one day believe because of them. Through the Scriptures we watched them walk with Jesus, run from him, and return to bring him glory. Just as Jesus needed their lives and words to be a testimony that showed him to us, the time has come for us to reveal Jesus to others. This means others will believe because of you.

> Just as surely as labor precedes natural birth, there are temporal battles before eternal dreams.

How does this happen? It is through God's glory. A very limited definition of his glory would be "God's full measure" or "his fullness." God gave his only begotten Son completely, and Jesus gave his life to the uttermost. There was never any portion withheld; nothing was kept on reserve. They were all in, completely one in purpose and expression. The goal of Jesus's prayer is for all of us to become one heart and mind so that the earth would once again see the glory of the Father and the Son, by the Spirit, in his bride.

Sadly, as I read these verses in John 17, I realized that even Jesus sometimes has to wait a long time for his prayers to be answered…because we are certainly not yet one.

We are all unique, so we can look, sound, feel, and smell different. Our expressions of worship can and should be varied, but if our life as a body is going to ultimately work, we *must* be *one*. The Message states John 17:23 this way:

> I in them and you in me.
> Then they'll be mature in this oneness,
> And give the godless *world evidence*
> That you've sent me and loved them
> In the *same way you've loved me.* (emphasis added)

If we're united, there's a chance the world might yet believe, but if we're divisive and divided, the odds are stacked against us! The current behavior of Christian cultures and communities has caused the inhabitants of the earth to question everything we stand for. Are we acting as though God sent his Son to save the lost world, or do we behave in a way that says it is all about us? Do we believe God loves them in the same way he loved Jesus? Is it hard to imagine that the Father loves us just as he loved his heavenly Son? I believe it is time we begin to act like the answer to Jesus's prayer. When this portrayal of *one* heart and mind is seen, here is what will happen:

> Father, I want those you gave me
> *To be with me, right where I am,*
> So they can see my glory, the splendor you gave me,
> *Having loved me*
> *Long before there ever was a world.* (verse 24, MSG, emphasis added)

Did you realize you were a gift the Father gave to his Son? It is as though the Father said, "Here, Jesus, hide this one away in your heart.

She is a treasure you will unearth later." This oneness is a mystery. How can we be with him when we are yet on earth? The answer: in Christ all become one. The godless world is searching for the evidence of Christ in us. I doubt they will see it until we realize the wonder of us in Christ. This realization will happen as we turn from ourselves *and look to him.*

The book of Ephesians explains this mystery best.

> In him we have redemption through his blood, the forgiveness of our trespasses, according to the riches of his grace, which he lavished upon us, in all wisdom and insight making known to us the mystery of his will, according to his purpose, which he set forth in Christ as a plan for the fullness of time, to unite all things in him, things in heaven and things on earth. (1:7–10)

This scripture again makes it clear that nothing was withheld; we were lavishly redeemed, forgiven, and graced with wisdom and insight to know both the mystery of his will and the purpose that was preset in Christ so that heaven and earth are united in him. Jesus came at the fullness of time, and we now walk the earth as time wanes. What might happen if we were one heart, one voice, one vision and purpose, one name, one kingdom, and one mandate to glorify Jesus? We would once again walk in a way that our weary earth would glimpse heaven.

Peace does not happen on its own. Peace is the fruit of the labor of God's sons and daughters.

> God blesses those who work for peace,
> for they will be called the children of God. (Matthew 5:9, NLT)

Division happens without any labor or contribution on our part. Division has been the natural course of this world since the fall of mankind. Unity and peace require intentional and strategic wisdom. We have to employ heaven's actions to counter our culture's initiatives.

Division never glorifies Jesus. Discord divides hearts, homes, voices, vision, purpose, and kingdoms. Division has many faces: pride, rage, wrath, contention, slander, gossip, curses, strife, bitterness and offense, witchcraft, and idolatry (see Galatians 5:19–21). These affronts gain access to our world when we live by carnal or brute human instincts. Even though divisiveness has many faces, it ultimately has a singular goal: our destruction.

> But if you have bitter jealousy and selfish ambition in your hearts,
> do not boast and be false to the truth. This is not the wisdom that
> comes down from above, but is earthly, unspiritual, demonic. For
> where jealousy and selfish ambition exist, there will be disorder
> and every vile practice. (James 3:14–16)

One of God's goals is to see the bride unified while understanding that he is jealous for her affections to be singularly his own. This means sometimes we must battle to become one. Jesus conquered death, hell, and the grave so that he could be one with us and we could be one with one another. Some of the most powerful relationships are forged when iron crosses iron and the resulting friction sharpens both. More often than not, you will encounter the greatest resistance to unity as soon as you intentionally decide to walk in unity.

Anytime you have one banner that functions to cover and empower

Fencing Fact

So irresistible was the lure of the sword that in the sixteenth century more noblemen (40,000) died from dueling (sword fighting to defend their honor) than in conventional warfare.

many, you will see division try to weave its spell within the ranks. I have seen this dynamic played out again and again in everything from friendships to churches. Attention is diverted from why you choose to walk together, and the focus shifts to how your needs aren't being met.

> *If you are going through hell, keep going.*
> —Winston Churchill

You don't set up camp in hell…you journey forward. An example of this is found in marriage. I don't know about you, but John and I didn't really fight in our season of dating. But after we got married and made a covenant of oneness before God, the dam broke loose. Not only is there fighting in marriages, but the very institution of marriage is under assault. What God defines we should not redefine, and what he joins we should not separate. Divorce is rampant as a generation has decided it is okay to cheat or leave if a couple feels they are no longer in love.

There are attacks on marriages and within marriages. I can't tell you how many times John and I have been shocked to hear of couples who apparently never fought in their marriages but are on the verge of divorce. We've learned that sometimes a lack of conflict *in* a marriage means you are not fighting *for* it. There are times you must battle to become one.

As you now know, dragons do not have their origin in mythical fantasy. Our references to dragons represent Satan, the ancient agent of spiritual death. Competition, slander, comparisons, and words that sow division are the dragon's language.

Just as the woman in the book of Revelation represents Israel, Mary, women, and the bride, the dragon represents Eden's serpent, Satan, leviathan, and all that seek to perversely twist God's character and words. The dragon is cunningly wicked and empowered by an anti-Christ spirit.

Before Adam and Eve could fulfill God's mandate to flourish in

Eden, the serpent pounced. He not only divided them but also divided their domain and removed them from the safety and nurture of a God-planted garden.

> *There is no neutral ground in the universe;*
> *every square inch, every split second, is claimed*
> *by God, and counter-claimed by Satan.*
> —C. S. LEWIS

He still crouches in the shadow of nightmares as he waits to pounce on all who would dare to dream. The dragon purposefully divides, demeans, and discourages any who would hope to rise up and move into the light by daring to dream in the dark.

Lovely One, if you dare to dream, you must be brave enough to fight.

From the vantage of a hero, look over your life and bravely look beyond both the people and the pain. How many times have you seen a serpent coiled in the shadows—hidden until it was time to pounce on your hopes and dreams?

When you were a little girl, maybe the dragon spoke words of fire that turned your hopes to ashes. Maybe he twisted words until you imagined his thoughts were your own. Did someone say you were ugly, fat, skinny, flat, stupid, too smart, short, or tall? Maybe your parents' love turned to hate and the former shelter of your home turned into an empty shell of a house. Maybe someone rode the dragon's wings in the night and came to you in the dark and touched you in places and ways that made you feel ashamed and dirty. Maybe as the serpent of shame slithered away, he hissed, "You asked for this; you wanted this; you are the one who made me do this."

In a strange way these initial words of blame have continued to surround women ever since Adam. When a guardian fails to protect, it is far easier to blame than to admit he has failed. It is true that the serpent beguiled Eve. But the magnificent Adam was not deceived. He willfully took what was not his to have. He wanted to be God without being under his rule. Even today, if a man steals a girl's or woman's virtue, it is easier to blame his actions on the influence of Eve rather than admit the truth: he wanted to steal her virtue and dominate her.

So as the millenniums have passed, has blaming the woman ever freed the man? No! Has blaming the man ever freed the woman? No! Jesus came to take the blame once and for all. Blame is always a distraction from what is truly going on. Any pain caused by people is just a shadow puppet of what is behind the scenes. We wrestle not with flesh and blood. There is a dragon in the shadows. He loves to warp the actions and perceptions of God's children. Both male and female are targeted for the serpent's theft. He wants to steal our birthright and malign our ability to bear God's image: "The thief comes only to steal and kill and destroy" (John 10:10).

When there is theft, death and destruction soon follow. Adam and Eve took what was not theirs to have, and immediately death gained entrance to our eternal garden. The earth soon followed this wake of destruction.

> Therefore, just as sin came into the world through one man, and death through sin, and so death spread to all men because all sinned. (Romans 5:12)

Jesus positioned us to flourish as we individually and corporately recover what was lost through theft, death, and destruction. As we become unified in purpose and flourish in our individual strengths, we could be likened once again to a glorious garden of which the Lord is the master gardener.

At that time GOD will unsheathe his sword,
 his merciless, massive, mighty sword.
He'll punish the serpent Leviathan as it flees,
 the serpent Leviathan thrashing in flight.
He'll kill that old dragon
 that lives in the sea.

"*At that same time,* a fine vineyard will appear.
 There's something to sing about!
I, GOD, tend it.
 I keep it well-watered.
I keep careful watch over it
 so that no one can damage it." (Isaiah 27:1–3, MSG,
  emphasis added)

As our God Most High fights, we flourish. As we his people flourish, our God strikes a killing blow. The battles in heaven are seen on earth, and the battles of earth do not escape the notice of heaven. We flourish when we are one with each other and with heaven's purpose.

Lovely One, the most powerful heroic thing you can do is to be fruitful. Repeatedly throughout the Scriptures, God refers to his people as vineyards, gardens, and fields. You are likened to a garden of his planting. Trees do not attack what is planted around them, nor do they imagine that the beauty of the flowers blooming in their shade detracts from the majesty of their strength. So let your roots go down deep and draw your strength from the unseen, and never allow the shadow of the dragon to blight the light of your future.

5

The Cross as a Sword

The Blood deals with what we have done,
whereas the Cross deals with what we are.
The Blood disposes of our sins, while the Cross
strikes at the root of our capacity for sin.

—Watchman Nee

When you think of the cross of Christ, no doubt many words come to mind, but *sword* is probably not one of them. Yet I believe the Cross has the power to speak differently to each of us as we journey through life's changing seasons. So let's pause and think of what the Cross currently means to you.

During an Easter season I posed a question to my avenues of social media, asking, "In one word what does the Cross mean to you?"

I was blessed with a deluge of answers. The collection of words used to describe the Cross included *love* (the most popular response by far), *grace, freedom, forgiveness,* and *redemption*—and ranged all the way to *Jesus, life, mercy, sacrifice,* and *a sense of overwhelming gratitude,* with many more beautiful definitions dancing between the words I have listed here.

First, let me be quick to say there is no single right, one-word definition of the Cross. The Cross bridged the gaping chasm between heaven and earth to reconcile God and humanity and went on to transform what appeared to be a horrific defeat into a stunning triumph. This empowering hope of transformation has spanned the ages. No other victory was compelling enough to reach back and light humankind's dark history while at the same time extending its rays into the future. Therefore, I doubt the breadth and meaning of all that happened on the cross could ever be captured and contained by our earthbound words. Yet the conquest of the Cross was more than timeless. It was eternal.

Close your eyes a moment, and imagine a wooden cross. I want you to see that what was once a beautiful living tree is now fashioned into a lifeless instrument of death. Stripped of all its branches and bark, the dead wood is roughly hewn and splintered. The harsh pieces are artificially joined to form a wooden cross, and when it is erected, it looks strangely like a sword with its point in the ground.

Now imagine Jesus, the Word made flesh and God's glorious Son, with his naked, beaten body stretched the length of this horrid sword blade. Nine-inch nails have anchored his hands to the cross-guard, and behind our master's head is the wooden sword's grip. Perhaps in heaven crosses and swords are one and the same.

Just as Adam stole the fruit of a forbidden tree and caused all within him to die, Jesus died on a barren tree and thus became its fruit that all in him might live.

Recently as I studied the book of Hebrews, I came across some familiar wording that held a new depth of meaning after my short expedition into the world of swords:

When God made his promise to Abraham, *he backed it to the hilt,* putting his own reputation on the line…. When God wanted to guarantee his promises, *he gave his word,* a rock-solid guarantee—

God *can't* break his word. And because *his word cannot change,* the promise is likewise unchangeable. (6:13, 17–18, MSG, emphasis added)

As I read this verse, suddenly a vivid image flashed across the window of my mind. I no longer saw the cross as a rugged tree of death. Instead it appeared as a wooden sword with its cruel point stabbed into our broken earth. I saw Jesus's body stretched upon the length or blade of the sword. His outstretched arms were spread wide across the cross-guard as if even in the agony of death his obedience welcomed us all.

What shifted my understanding was my study of swords and their terminology, which brought a new understanding of the phrase *to the hilt.* Before my research I only thought in terms of this phrase's figurative meaning, which expresses "to the very limit, completely," and "nothing lacking." But now I realize there is a literal meaning of *to the hilt* as well, because the word *hilt* refers to the anatomy of a sword.

The hilt is the sword's handle, which begins where the blade ends. The hilt includes the sword's cross-guard, pommel, and grip. When put together, all these components are known as the hilt.

When a sword is driven into an opponent all the way to the hilt, there is little chance of the victim escaping death. The blade will only be drawn back when the adversary feels his victory is certain. Stabbing someone all the way to the hilt is a cruel move made by aggressive opponents who enjoy close contact with their victim's pain. The aggressor is certain of his victory because he has completely closed the distance between them. There is no safety gap between the enemy and himself.

Through the offering of his Son, Jesus, God used the cross as a sword to kill the hostility between God and man.

On the cross God kept his promise to Abraham to the uttermost.

Who Was Responsible for the Cross?

Often I hear people say that Satan crucified our Lord of glory, but the following parable reveals something tragically different. It begins as the story of a master builder who planted a vineyard, fenced it in, dug a wine press, built a tower, and leased the land to tenants. When the season of fruit came, he sent individual servants, whom the tenants beat, killed, and stoned. So then the master sent more servants, and these were abused and killed as well. Finally the master sent his son in the hope that the tenants would respect his son and give him his due. Watch who the players are as this story unfolds:

> "When the tenants saw the son, they said to themselves, 'This
> is the heir. Come, let us kill him and have his inheritance.' And
> they took him and threw him out of the vineyard and killed him.
> When therefore the owner of the vineyard comes, what will he do
> to those tenants?" They said to him, "He will put those wretches
> to a miserable death and let out the vineyard to other tenants who
> will give him the fruits in their seasons."
>
> Jesus said to them, "Have you never read in the Scriptures:
>
> > " 'The stone that the builders rejected
> >   has become the cornerstone;
> > this was the Lord's doing,
> >   and it is marvelous in our eyes'?
>
> Therefore I tell you, the kingdom of God will be taken away from
> you and given to a people producing its fruits. And the one who
> falls on this stone will be broken to pieces; and when it falls on
> anyone, it will crush him."

When the chief priests and the Pharisees heard his parables, *they perceived that he was speaking about them.* (Matthew 21:38–45, emphasis added)

In this parable God the Father is the master, the prophets and kings of old are the servants he sent, Jesus is the son, and the priests and Pharisees are the tenants. Later as these events were unfolding, Jesus reminded his disciples of what was about to happen:

"You know that after two days the Passover is coming, and the Son of Man will be delivered up to be crucified."
Then the chief priests and the elders of the people gathered in the palace of the high priest, whose name was Caiaphas, and plotted together in order to arrest Jesus by stealth and kill him. (Matthew 26:2–4)

Isaiah and David prophesied that God's chosen people would kill his one and only begotten Son. The religious leaders thought that by killing God's Son they would get to steal his inheritance, but instead they became his inheritance.

None of the rulers of this age understood this, for if they had, they would not have crucified the Lord of glory. (1 Corinthians 2:8, emphasis added)

What blindsided each and every ruler of that age? They could not see the transforming and triumphant power of the Cross.
This designation of rulers could encompass everyone, from the religious and political powers at the time of Christ to the very Prince of Darkness, who pulled their strings through his whispered innuendos and network of demonic minions.

I wonder if Satan hoped the murder of God's only begotten Son by the very ones he'd called "chosen" would ensure for us God's eternal wrath? After all, stealing a shared fruit and grasping at equality with God had earned Adam banishment from the Garden of Eden. Would not the murder of God's Son then surely be the end of us all—in Satan's thinking?

The apostle Paul prefaced his insightful statement above (1 Corinthians 2:8) by contrasting the wisdom of the Spirit and the wisdom of man:

> Yet among the mature we do impart wisdom, although it is not
> a wisdom of this age or of the rulers of this age, who are doomed
> to pass away. But we impart a secret and hidden wisdom of
> God, which *God decreed before the ages* for our glory. (verses 6–7,
> emphasis added)

God's wisdom was at work before our foolishness came into play. Before time was birthed, God was thinking of you. The Cross was woven into heaven's mysterious tapestry of eternal wisdom. This magnificent rendering of his love continuously unfolds and reveals itself.

Just think of it, Jesus was our lamb *before* sheep were created. He was the Savior of our earth before the world was founded. If all this wasn't enough, we were chosen "in him" before creation to be made spotless!

> …even as he *chose us in him before the foundation of the world,*
> that we should be holy and blameless before him. (Ephesians 1:4,
> emphasis added)

Before the Garden of Eden was seeded, we were planted in him. Before Adam and Eve were put out of the garden, we were securely hidden in Christ. Before our sins were as scarlet, God washed them white as snow.

I don't think the rulers of that age were particularly surprised that

Jesus rose from the dead. They had seen the dead raised before, and Jesus had told everyone he would rise after three days. I think Satan knew resurrection was part of the plan. What Satan and the rulers may not have realized was that as Jesus came up out of the grave, we rose with him! Scripture tells us,

> I have been *crucified with Christ*. It is no longer I who live, but
> Christ who lives in me. And the life I now live in the flesh I live
> by faith in the Son of God, who loved me and gave himself for
> me. (Galatians 2:20, emphasis added)

He didn't just take our place; he gave us…his. We have his life, his name, his words, his authority, and his promise. Not one of us was alive when our Christ was crucified. But that doesn't matter, because even before time began we were chosen in Christ Jesus…predestined as children of God. Just as in Adam all have sinned, in Christ all are forgiven. Our lives hidden in Christ are mysteries he longs to continually unveil.

You see, the Cross was always part of the plan. It was not a backup plan that was set into motion when Adam and Eve failed. It was the fail-safe. Each day Jesus lived to express the Father's heart, will, and nature to the lost inhabitants of earth—"For *in him we live, and move, and have our being;* as certain also of your own poets have said, For we are also his offspring" (Acts 17:28, KJV, emphasis added).

God's wisdom was at work before our foolishness came into play.

He is our life, our author, and the one who changes us. By studying the definition of each of these words, I can expand this verse's meaning and shed a bit more light on this concept of "in him." Because of him, we no longer exist in Adam. We live in Christ and are seated with him as we walk on earth.

The death of Jesus should have come as no surprise, but apparently the aftermath was a shock. Even though Jesus repeatedly told both his intimate friends and his fiercest critics that he would suffer and die and after three days rise again, they just could not, would not hear of it.

> From then on Jesus began to tell his disciples *plainly* that it was necessary for him to go to Jerusalem, and that he would suffer many terrible things at the hands of the elders, the leading priests, and the teachers of religious law. He would be killed, but on the third day he would be raised from the dead. (Matthew 16:21, NLT, emphasis added).

This wasn't one of those times when Jesus spoke in parables so that only "those who had ears could hear" (see Matthew 13:10–17). Jesus told his disciples clearly and repeatedly that in the near future he would intentionally journey to Jerusalem, where the leaders of his people would reject him. This turn of events would result in horrible suffering, death, and resurrection. As you know, Peter went so far as to pull Jesus aside and rebuke him for saying as much.

> Peter took him aside and began to reprimand him for saying such things. "Heaven forbid, Lord," he said. "This will never happen to you!"
>
> Jesus turned to Peter and said, "Get away from me, Satan! You are a dangerous trap to me. You are seeing things merely from a human point of view, not from God's." (Matthew 16:22–23, NLT)

There is so much happening in this interchange. First, don't you find it rather odd that in a conversation in which Peter has just evoked heaven and called Jesus "Lord," Jesus would look at Peter and speak to Satan?

Then there is the revelation that Peter's impassioned assurance of safety and protection for his beloved leader is actually an invitation to the entrapment of death. And last, but certainly far from the least shocking, there is the disclosure that at times Satan and humans share common points of view.

To bring some clarity, let's do the math, because apparently heaven and earth balance their equations very differently.

- By the Rules of Earth (Human and Satanic) Equation:
  Rejection + Suffering + Death = Loss of Power and Defeat
- By the Rules of Heaven (Jesus and God) Equation:
  Rejection + Suffering + Death = Unlimited Power and Victory

It was a move so illogical and counterintuitive that even though it was completely explained, it was totally unexpected. This victory was not Jesus's alone, because his triumph became ours. Nowhere is the power of this transformation more evident than in the life of Peter. The ear-hacking former Christ-denier, whose voice sounded like Satan's, is later seen boldly confronting the very ones who used to make him cower.

> "Let all the house of Israel therefore know for certain that God has
> made him both Lord and Christ, this Jesus whom you crucified."
>
> Now when they heard this they were cut to the heart, and
> said to Peter and the rest of the apostles, "Brothers, what shall we
> do?" And Peter said to them, "Repent and be baptized every one
> of you in the name of Jesus Christ for the forgiveness of your sins,
> and you will receive the gift of the Holy Spirit." (Acts 2:36–38)

We were saved, forgiven, healed, loved, graced, empowered, and re-stored "in Christ." Just as "in Christ" God caught us before we fell. The mystery and wonder of it will forever unfold.

Eternity alone will reveal the brilliance of the Cross.

Before there was an adversary, a garden, a man, a woman, and a serpent, there was an answer. Before there was a war, there was a victory. Before there was even the concept of a game, the Cross was the game-changing agent. The Cross was the means that facilitated the purpose for which Jesus was born. It was the dead tree that brought us all back to life. God lifted us in Christ long before we stumbled. He made a way for us before we lost ours. He loved and knew us first, long before we ever knew him. God covered us before we realized we were naked and made us whole before we knew we were broken. Our Giver of All Life changed the Cross into a Tree of Life.

Fencing Fact

Emotions that are the most detrimental to fencing are anger and fear.

Why the instrument of the cross? Over the course of life, I've learned that God allows human cruelty and depravity to reveal our deep, desperate need of him. My study of sword fighting may have revealed one of many reasons.

The Croisé

In my research I found it fascinating that a classic fencing or sword fighting move is called the croisé, a French word that means "to cross or to take the blade." This move works by leveraging a hostile opponent's aggression back upon him, and in the process the foe is disarmed.

Here's a description of the move: "It is the mechanics of the croisé that makes it work; adding muscle to the equation just overbalances the whole thing and destroys your ability to effectively place your point where it should be going. The croisé works especially well against highly aggressive fencers, because it negates their energy, turning both their brawn and their belligerence back against them."[4]

As fencing turned into a sport and moved from Italy and France to Great Britain, the English simplified the name of this move to "the cross." Think of it! What happened on the cross? Our magnificent Savior took the blade when his side was pierced, but on the cross he took upon himself the hostility of *all the ages*. What should have been devastating proved to be disarming.

> On the cross
> God leveraged
> all that he was
> for all that we
> could be.

The power of the croisé, or the cross, comes from leverage. When executed with proper form and employed without hesitation, the opponent runs upon your blade. This is not a move that requires a heavy hand; in fact, it is best done with the gentlest of touches.

On the cross God leveraged all that he was for all that we could be. Nearly three centuries before the birth of Christ, the brilliant Greek mathematician Archimedes hypothesized about the power of leverage: "Give me a lever, and I will move the world."[5]

One of the equations for leverage is Moment = Force x Vertical Distance.[6] In a moment the Cross spanned the unfathomable distance between God and humanity and overcame every force of hostility.

The cross was God's lever, and the earth became his fulcrum in the moment Christ gave his life to save the world.

Jesus offered no resistance as the divine transfer happened. He yielded his soul to God and his body to his enemies.

> *The name of Jesus is the one lever*
> *that lifts the world.*
> —AUTHOR UNKNOWN

Just as the name of Jesus lifts the world, the Cross of Christ was the lever that saved the world.

Ultimately sword fighting is not a contest of strength; it is one of finesse and strategic endurance. Jesus endured the cross and bore the force of all our sins to realize his purpose: "The reason the Son of God *appeared* was to destroy the works of the devil" (1 John 3:8, emphasis added).

Our glorious Lord Jesus, Son of the Most High, appeared on our scene so that he could dismantle the kingdom the devil had built. Jesus is Immanuel—God with us, invisible but invincible. Though he seems to have disappeared, he actually increased in ascendency, for his presence covers us all. Before his ascension he was limited by the restraints of his human appearance; now he surrounds us by his Spirit (see Matthew 28:20).

I believe Christ wants us to carry on his work so that, just as he revealed the Father, we are to glorify the Son. Every action we choose should serve to draw others near.

> But now in Christ Jesus you who once were far off have been brought near by the blood of Christ. For he himself is our peace, who has made us both one and has broken down in his flesh the dividing wall of hostility by abolishing the law of commandments expressed in ordinances, that he might create in himself one new man in place of the two, so making peace, and might reconcile us both to God in one body through the cross, thereby killing the hostility. (Ephesians 2:13–16)

The Cross eradicated every trace of hostility between God and humanity, and through Jesus's blood and broken body, we are all made one. In Christ, men and women are one flesh. In Christ, Jews and Gentiles are woven into one vine. In Christ, the Old Testament and New Testament saints become one cloud of witnesses.

As I read these verses in Ephesians, my heart is rent by the depth of their might and beauty. All that was accomplished by the obedience of Jesus awes me. Jesus made a way for us to be in the world but no longer of it, because we move through this earth in him. In Christ, we are at once contained and uncontainable.

All the good will that was stripped away in Eden was recovered in him. As awesome as life in Eden must have been, our life in him will ultimately be far better. He covered us with far more than a withering fig leaf or a dead lambskin; he robed us in his living righteousness and transformed us from the inside out. We are not merely a skeletal framework of bone of his bone. He layered us with the tender flesh of his flesh. He took away our hardened hearts and gave us new hearts fashioned out of his lineage. Then he filled us with the same Spirit that raised Christ from the dead so that every decaying area of our lives could be regenerated and redeemed.

> The Spirit of God, who raised Jesus from the dead, lives in you.
> And just as God raised Christ Jesus from the dead, he will give
> life to your mortal bodies by this same Spirit living within you.
> (Romans 8:11, NLT)

He became like us so we could be like him. In him a great mystery is expressed, and somehow we all become one.

> I will give them one heart, and a new spirit I will put within them.
> I will remove the heart of stone from their flesh and give them
> a heart of flesh, that they may walk in my statutes and keep my
> rules and obey them. And they shall be my people, and I will be
> their God. (Ezekiel 11:19–20)

In Christ, the many share one heart. In him, man and woman become one. Through his sacrifice, Christ and his bride become one. In him, all that was divided can become unified. The utterly obedient sacrifice of our Christ saved us to the uttermost. The Cross has the power to unify all who are willing to embrace it.

In Christ, the far off, lost, and wandering come near.

Scapegoat

Did you know that in the ancient times when Aaron was priest, two goats were brought before the altar as an offering? One was killed as a sacrifice for sin; the other was designated as the scapegoat, and it was not killed. The priest transferred the sin of God's people to its trembling frame. Then it was released. Like Cain, this goat was marked and doomed to wander the wilderness in shame (see Leviticus 16:10).

This goat was now a shunned outsider. It no longer had any part in the flock. The shepherd no longer provided it pleasant fields or protection. If the scapegoat came near anyone, it was driven away. It rested uneasy and alone at night, cold without the warmth of others. In the daylight it wandered in the arid heat. The scapegoat spent the balance of its days searching for water and food, at the mercy of ravenous beasts.

Have you ever felt like a scapegoat? Maybe you were blamed, shunned, isolated, and rejected. Burdened by sin and guilt, maybe you have wandered in a wilderness. Maybe even now you lie down each night alone and in cold fear. Did you try to come in from "the outside" and they wouldn't let you? Did your family blame and push you away? Were you pressed to the outer band of your circle of friends or forced from the shelter of a church building?

No matter! In Jesus, space was made for you. All of us are flawed, but he is flawless. There is no longer a need for scapegoats, because Jesus took all the sin. The blood of Christ brought in all who had wandered and purged any remnant of shame that tried to isolate us and keep us as scapegoats.

Even as he died, he could have released judgment, but instead he said, "Father, forgive them; for they know not what they do" (Luke 23:34, KJV). With these words the imprint of God in his Son overrode the pattern of blame Adam and Eve had set in motion. The blood of Adam's son Abel rightly called out and named his brother a murderer. Jesus's blood called his brothers forgiven. This is why the Bible says the blood of Jesus speaks of better things: "You have come...to Jesus the mediator of a new covenant, and to the sprinkled blood that speaks a better word than the blood of Abel" (Hebrews 12:23–24, NIV).

The better word was "Father, forgive them." He chose to be marked with our destruction rather than mark us for the destruction that we deserved.

> Yet it was our weaknesses he carried;
> > it was our sorrows that weighed him down.
> And we thought his troubles were a punishment from God,
> > a punishment for his own sins!
> But he was pierced for our rebellion,
> > crushed for our sins.
> He was beaten so we could be whole.
> > He was whipped so we could be healed.
> All of us, like sheep, have strayed away.
> > We have left God's paths to follow our own.
> Yet the LORD laid on him
> > the sins of us all. (Isaiah 53:4–6, NLT)

Jesus did nothing to deserve punishment, and we did nothing to deserve his sacrifice. He was rejected, betrayed, pierced, crushed, beaten, whipped, oppressed, and then crucified.

Only a God who is love would give his Spirit to those who repented of murdering his Son. They thought the cross was Jesus's end; they had no idea it was their beginning. The cross is the sword of love.

After more than three decades of studying the Scriptures, sometimes I wonder if I even begin to understand this wonder that is the Cross. It is not a symbol of power; it is the measure of all power. What was death to our Christ became life abundant to us.

Our Jesus is God's Word and is, was, and will be his promise unchangeable: "Jesus Christ the same yesterday, and to day, and for ever" (Hebrews 13:8, KJV).

•   •   •

The Cross is the ultimate assurance of every promise kept. It is a sword that slays every last remnant of hostility between heaven and earth, just as surely as it is a sword that transforms us through the surgery of the Word. The Cross was your hope even before you realized you were hopeless, the answer before you realized there was a problem. The Cross symbolizes God's faithfulness while it expresses his faith in us. Through the Cross we are equipped to walk in him.

PART TWO

TRAINED

6

Becoming a Warrior

Struggle is strengthening. Battling with evil
gives us the power to battle evil even more.

—Ossie Davis

I believe God has awakened his daughters to be more than soldiers. He is calling us to be warriors. Therefore, in this chapter I will be using some military terms, but understand I am not referring to our nation's servicemen and servicewomen when I contrast the nature of a soldier with the nature of a warrior.

As I waded through books on swordsmanship and fencing, I quickly realized there is a vast array of motives for taking up arms and engaging in battle.

There are angry terrorists who fight in cruel and underhanded ways for their desperate and ill-begotten causes. Then there are the mercenaries who love to fight, so much so that they need no personal cause, and their allegiance is for sale to the highest bidder. On the other end of the spectrum are soldiers who are employed and serve under the command of an army.

Finally, there are those who are warriors.

"Warrior" is a way of life, and many of the battles they fight are with enemies unseen. All warriors must be skilled in something the ancient samurai called *the way of the warrior,* an approach to life that embraces *freedom without fear.* I can't think of a better posture for us to assume. If we rearrange these words, we capture the stance of a captive: *fear without freedom.*

Sadly, fear without freedom is becoming the new normal for many. As warrior-daughters, we have the opportunity to lose our lives and gain God's. This means we are free to choose the path of freedom without fear, because our Lord settled the issues of death and life on the cross.

This position is unique to the warrior. The samurai named their swords because they believed each sword had a spirit attached to it that gave it power. This practice evolved into the worship of swords. Conversely, we do not need a sword with a spirit, because we have the sword of the Spirit! Directed by the Word of God, we use the name of Jesus and worship with our lives as we lift his Word above our will.

The terrorist is driven by fear, the mercenary or soldier of fortune is motivated by greed, and even enlisted soldiers *must* obey commands. But the warrior has a choice. Honoring what is godly and noble is often the rite of passage when a soldier becomes a warrior.

Lovely One, I am sure you recognize you have been born into a season of upheaval, conflict, and war. Battles rage on every front. Sadly these attacks range from the intimate atrocity of child abuse and abandonment in what should be the refuge and safety of a home to insidious networks that traffic in as many as twenty-seven million humans for sex and labor.[7] In addition to these secret terrors, we live in a day of open threats. We stand on the sidelines as nations challenge each other with the constant threat of depersonalized war.

Because this assault occurs on numerous fronts, involves so many, and threatens so much, we cannot limit our fight to merely the immediate battle before us. Our goal should be to win each battle in such a manner that we ultimately and gloriously win the war. This approach requires strategy, intuition, vision, wisdom, patience, persistence, tenacity, a unified voice, and concerted effort.

To illustrate the point, imagine a virtual video game. How do you fare if your goal is simply to win the present level? As I understand it, a player with that mind-set will not fare very well or last in the game for very long. Mind you, I am completely incapable of playing such games, but my boys have achieved some level of mastery. And after limited observation, I've noticed the goal isn't just to run through the gauntlet on one level quickly. There is always something to be picked up or learned at the current level that you will need at a later time.

I watch as my sons maneuver and take risks to get certain articles hidden within the confines of the course at a given level. Each of these items has a unique value, but the need for these items is not usually immediate. More often than not they are collected for their future value.

Stepping away from the example of the game and back into the very real paths of our world, you should never doubt that what *seems* a small or insignificant decision or gesture now may very well open a passageway or even empower you in the future.

Here is why doing the small things well is so crucial. It isn't just our actions that move ahead with us into the future; the lessons we learn on each path journey with us as well. Understand that the secret you chose to keep or your act of unseen loyalty from *last season* may very well protect you in your *next season.*

Warriors move through life with foresight, and they understand there is an opportunity to build skill and strength with every challenge.

> *It is not a field of a few acres of ground, but a cause, that*
> *we are defending, and whether we defeat the enemy in one*
> *battle, or by degrees, the consequences will be the same.*
> —THOMAS PAINE

Wars should never be about dirt; they should be about principles. The American revolutionaries took up arms to fight the injustice of their day. It was a costly and cruel war with many soldiers and warriors dying on both sides. But this is not the type of war we are waging. Our war is not about injustice; it's about God versus Satan. Ultimately, you are part of an ancient struggle between darkness and light.

The Enemy's Target

Returning to a study of Scripture, the first time we find the word *warrior* mentioned, it is paired with such adjectives as *heroic, great,* and *mighty:* "Cush was also the ancestor of Nimrod, who was the first *heroic warrior on earth,*" (Genesis 10:8, NLT, emphasis added).

The designation of "first...on earth" lets us know that heroic warriors already existed in heaven, and Nimrod was but the first human warrior revealed on earth. Our troubled world is a fallen, shadowed reflection of the exalted, glorious heavens. Therefore, it should not surprise us that conflicts waged long ago in heaven would spread and exert themselves on earth. Just such a war in the heavens is described in the book of Revelation:

Now *war arose in heaven,* Michael and his angels fighting against
the dragon. And the dragon and his angels fought back, but
he was defeated, and there was no longer any place for them in
heaven. (Revelation 12:7–8, emphasis added)

This passage reveals the name of one of heaven's mightiest warriors,
the archangel Michael. In this war the dragon and his forces are not only
defeated; they are displaced. The ancient battle moves to different soil,
and the dragon rages against God's daughters.

"But woe to you, O earth and sea, for the devil has come down to
you in great wrath, because he knows that his time is short!"
   And when *the dragon* saw that he had been thrown down to
the earth, he *pursued the woman* who had given birth to the male
child. But the woman was given the two wings of the great eagle
so that she might fly from the serpent into the wilderness, to the
place where she is to be nourished for a time, and times, and half
a time. The serpent poured water like a river out of his mouth
after the woman, to sweep her away with a flood. (verses 12–15,
emphasis added)

There is so much prophetic symbolism here that I would not dare
to say I understand all of it. This passage is ripe with both spiritual and
literal meaning, but wrapped in all the mystery, there is a clarion truth:
this devil-dragon-serpent is relentless in his pursuit of the destruction of
"the woman." Bible commentators believe in this passage the woman
represents Israel. Then later the dragon takes his war to her children.

Then the *dragon became furious with the woman* and went off
to *make war on the rest of her offspring,* on those who *keep the*

commandments of God and *hold to the testimony of Jesus.* (verse 17, emphasis added)

Make no mistake, Satan wants to undermine God and destroy his children. *Church* is a feminine term, which includes both male and female, but his fury is repeatedly leveled against *the woman.* First there was Eve, then Sarah, then Israel, then Mary. Now his venomous attacks are leveled at the bride. He has a longstanding history of hatred toward women, and there is no surer way to wound a woman than to attack her children. And who are the children of this woman? *All* who keep God's commands and hold to the testimony of Jesus. Does this include you?

Lovely One, you already know you are a target. You might as well choose to be a warrior hero.

The Original Warrior

The next time our term *warrior* is mentioned in the Scriptures, it is a revelation of the God Most High: "The LORD is a warrior; Yahweh is his name!" (Exodus 15:3, NLT).

Yahweh, our High and Holy Father, is the original warrior. The Lord of all is not a part-time father, part-time soldier. Our God Most High is both and more. He is our Almighty Warrior-Father, and we are his daughters—bone of his bone and flesh of his flesh. So it stands to reason that woven within our fabric is the DNA of a warrior.

I want us to be able to move forward with a decisive step and true sense of clarity. You are at once a daughter and a warrior. There are even more poetic names given to this designation, like warrior-princess or princess-warrior. I like all of them. Feel free to choose the one that suits you best. In this chapter I want to paint a picture of what a warrior-daughter looks like by comparing and contrasting the concepts of warrior and soldier.

The first contrast is evident in the way each role starts: warriors are called, but soldiers are hired. You can be a warrior without ever enlisting. The need of the moment calls warriors forth and beckons their hearts to war. Look around you. Is there not a cause? Warriors are not hired to be part of something. There is a quickening within them that joins them to the cause.

While most soldiers are paid, true warriors are made.

You are not a civilian who has been drafted or hired to be part of a passing battle in a distant land. No organization can assign you rank, because you are a royal daughter of the King—handpicked for a purpose. There is nothing impersonal about this battle; it is an all-out war on your family.

> *Let* the *king* be enthralled by your beauty; *honor* him, for he is
> your *lord*. (Psalm 45:11, NIV, emphasis added)

Throughout my study of swords and fencing, one theme remained constant: *honor*. The word *let* in the scripture above implies there could be a way to disallow or deny the king's enjoyment of your beauty. I believe the main way we deny our King access to our beauty is through dishonor. Sadly, we live in a day when dishonor is not only rampant but celebrated.

Our present culture is more likely to encourage women to *dishonor* their bodies with immodesty, impropriety, obesity, and other eating disorders than to *honor* their bodies through modesty, propriety, and moderation. What were once commonly held as virtues—integrity, a good name, and a sterling reputation—are no longer celebrated in our culture's songs. You are more likely to hear of lewd dance moves, expensive accessories, fast cars, and women flocking to men who flash cash in a club. Apparently in this pseudoworld of rappers and bling, the arrogant, indecent, unscrupulous, and greedy feel entitled to our respect.

Seduction has been substituted for beauty, and the power of manipulation is rewarded over the influence of wisdom. Foolishness no longer needs to call to us from the streets when its message and music can easily find its way into our homes.

My husband always says honor begins in the heart and works its way out until it is expressed through our actions. Likewise, I believe the way of the warrior-daughter begins with her heart. Therefore, she zealously guards it by guarding her mind. This means giving heed to what is heard and said as well as what is seen and done. The distorted thread of dishonor wants to weave itself into the fabric of our lives and taint all that would be beautiful.

Our Warrior-King is beautiful.

His very image is beyond compare.

The wondrous span of creation captures a mere fragment of his beauty.

The mighty ocean, soaring skies, and majestic mountains declare the powerful, immeasurable, enduring beauty of his strength.

Each and every living thing—from plants to animals—is an irresistible revelation of the fact that our God is gorgeous!

He lovingly formed his sons and daughters to carry more of his majesty, glory, and beauty than any other creation.

We are his masterpiece.

That is why it is all the more tragic when we behave in ways that dishonor his right to reign in and over our lives. When we do not honor him by honoring others, his reflection in us is distorted. Even the world knows we are supposed to be loving and therefore lovely.

As daughters, we bear our Father's image. When we love him with all our hearts, that includes the meditations of our minds and the fullness of our strength. But when we mar the counsel of his Word through willful disobedience, the compelling beauty of the Holy Spirit's transforming power in our lives is lost in translation to a world that would love to see a people made new.

I've learned in my research that there is no way to separate a true warrior from honor, because warriors are honor-bound to something higher than themselves. The mighty samurai lived this discipline, and the medieval knights practiced chivalry. Honor meant they complied with stringent codes that required commitment and discipline. Knights pledged their loyalty to uphold the reign of earthly kings. In exchange for their fealty, they were granted lands and titles. This often meant they were required to die on the battlefield.

We do not serve an earthly, mortal king whose justice is measured in earthly rewards. Ultimately, God is our reward. One day his wisdom, mercy, and justice will awe the nations for eons. This is our King, the One who is worthy beyond our human measure and beyond our human words to describe.

Our generous King knew that we would fail a stringent code of ethics and that none of us was capable of earning a place of honor. So instead he accepted us through adoption and gave us the honor of his name. He knew we could not find our way, so he taught us his royal ways by sending his Son into our world. Our stunning Father-King has given us his life so we can escape our certain sentence of death and share in his kingdom that is to come and have access to his authority and power now.

If there ever was a people with a reason to be honor-bound, we should be. So why is there so much dishonor among his people? Have we become weary soldiers rather than fiery warriors? I honestly do not have an answer to these questions, but I do believe we can be the answer to the problem. We have the power to individually and collectively change this trend.

Soldiers are trained. Warriors are tempered.

Becoming a Warrior

Are you ready to sign on to being more than a soldier? If so, please understand your warrior preparation process will look quite a bit different. All soldiers are trained, but in addition to being trained, as a warrior, you will also be tempered. I warn you, the process of tempering is not pleasant or quick. (More on this in the next chapter)

Any soldier can see what the enemy is doing and then report his movements. No discernment is needed to see what is obvious. On the other hand, warriors are leaders who also perceive what God is doing in the realm of the unseen. A soldier may say, "Look, we are surrounded by chaos and problems." A warrior knows God is in control, and his army is already poised for a counterattack.

Fencing Fact

Bad fencing is emotional, is unrepeatable, is brutal and harmful, looks only for results, is filled with pointless movement.

In Scripture there is a great example of this when the Syrian king sent his army of soldiers against the warrior-prophet Elisha. It didn't matter what move the king of Syria made or how carefully he set up an ambush, because the prophet Elisha had spiritual insight, and he forewarned the king of Israel. Exasperated, the Syrian king decided to lay hold of Elisha. During the night this annoyed king surrounded the entire city of Dothan, where the prophet resided. When Elisha's servant woke the next morning, he was overwhelmed. He explained the situation to Elisha: they were surrounded by horses, chariots, and an impressive fighting force, which left them with no means of escape. Like a good soldier, he reported the enemy's position. Now listen to the warrior's answer to this news:

> He said, "Do not be afraid, for those who are with us are more than those who are with them." Then Elisha prayed and said, "O LORD, please open his eyes that he may see." So the LORD opened the eyes of the young man, and he saw, and behold, the mountain was full of horses and chariots of fire all around Elisha. (2 Kings 6:16–17)

Fear blinds. But there are always more who are with us than we know. The warrior-daughter carries this encouragement within her breast: "What then shall we say to these things? If God is for us, who can be against us?" (Romans 8:31).

This scripture poses both a question and an answer. For greater is he (Jesus) who is in us than he (Satan) that is in the world (see 1 John 4:4). Sometimes this assurance appears to us as an encampment of flaming chariots; other times it is an inextinguishable hope that burns within.

Warriors are driven by an internal eternal mandate. Their response is ordered from within. This means they will give all that is in their power to give. There is an overflow in their response, because children should do more than hired servants. Soldiers follow orders to the letter. Yet sometimes these orders are followed without the passionate heart of their commander. The letter kills, but the Spirit knows how to give life.

> *Good men must not obey the laws too well.*
> —RALPH WALDO EMERSON

Returning to the story of our warrior-prophet Elisha, we find that God has blinded the enemy in response to Elisha's prayer, and Elisha has led the entire army into the court of Israel's king. The king was overjoyed to see his enemies delivered to his doorstep, and he asked Elisha for his permission to strike and kill all of them. Elisha answered:

> Not on your life!… You didn't lift a hand to capture them, and now you're going to kill them? No sir, make a feast for them and send them back to their master. (2 Kings 6:22, MSG)

The Syrian attacks against Israel stopped after this.

A soldier might have slaughtered the very ones that the warrior fed. The slaughter would not have ended the attacks but would have escalated the tension and expanded into a more hateful war. Elisha exemplified the words of Christ (see Luke 6:27) before they were even spoken. God's Spirit leads his warrior-prophets. Even the king looked to Elisha for strategy. While following the dictates of men to the letter, soldiers may drive, dictate, and slaughter. Conversely, warriors will lead and irresistibly compel others to join the cause.

Soldiers have an enlisted mind-set. They know they have signed up for just so many years, and most intend to do no more or less. They hold their position, but their position has no hold on them; they serve so they can retire. The warrior never retires. *Warrior* is a status or posture one carries throughout life.

King David was a warrior his entire life. He won his first battle against a bear and a lion:

> David said to Saul, "Your servant used to keep sheep for his father. And when there came a lion, or a bear, and took a lamb from the flock, I went after him and struck him and delivered it out of his mouth. And if he arose against me, I caught him by his beard and struck him and killed him." (1 Samuel 17:34–35)

David had fought and won this battle in private. His sole witnesses were sheep, stars, and God. His brothers may have questioned whether this confrontation with a bear and a lion even happened. You may have private battles of your own. You may have won victories no one knew how to celebrate. Or perhaps like David, you were alone and no one believes the confrontation occurred. Be patient: God never wastes a private victory. There is a day on earth or in heaven when the victory will be celebrated! This day came for David when he proved himself a warrior by publicly killing Goliath.

> Then David said to the Philistine, "You come to me with a sword
> and with a spear and with a javelin, but I come to you in the
> name of the LORD of hosts, the God of the armies of Israel, whom
> you have defied. *This day the LORD will deliver you into my hand,*
> and I will strike you down and cut off your head." (verses 45–46,
> emphasis added)

Can't you almost see David running, gaining speed with every step, fearlessly propelled by the strength of the name of his God? But I wonder what might have happened if David had chosen not to kill the lion or the bear. What if he had decided one sheep wasn't worth risking his life? A soldier would resolve to keep a better watch in the future, but to a warrior the future is now. A warrior recovers all. Never imagine that what you do for others or what you do in private doesn't matter. It counts more than we know. God watches how we steward what is not our own before he entrusts us with more.

A warrior doesn't weigh the odds when right needs to triumph over wrong. It takes the heart of a warrior to pursue a lion with a lamb in its mouth. The battles we win in private position us to slay giants in public.

I believe David's greatest warrior moments were captured in the stories of whom he let live. For me, his greatest victories were not in the season when the women sang, "David has killed his ten thousands" (see 1 Samuel 18:7). His true greatness as a warrior was revealed in a much smaller number—three. David proved himself a true warrior when he refused to kill Saul in self-defense and when he didn't kill Nabal and Shimei, both of whom were maligning him. By sparing their lives and making room for God's justice, he proved himself a king.

True warrior-daughters fear the Lord and therefore joyously worship and obey him.

Warriors understand they carry a sword for the sake of justice, not judgment. A soldier would have killed them all. It is what soldiers do; they are trained to take lives. Warriors do more. They give and take life to establish a legacy. Warriors fight according to the will of God, while soldiers war for the will of the people.

Saul was the people's king, and he was also their soldier. Soldiers serve the army, which is the very public voice of the people. He proved this designation when he allowed the people to compel him, and he lost the legacy God would have established.

> Saul said to Samuel, "I have sinned, for I have transgressed the commandment of the LORD and your words, because I feared the people and obeyed their voice." (1 Samuel 15:24)

You will inevitably serve whom you fear. Warriors obey God.

> For the LORD, the Most High, is to be feared,
>   a great king over all the earth. (Psalm 47:2)

True warrior-daughters fear the Lord and therefore joyously worship and obey him. Soldiers fear man and therefore obey the people. All warriors know they ultimately answer to an unseen Lord who is the maker of heaven and earth.

Saul's Warrior-Son

The soldier-king Saul did have a warrior-son named Jonathan, who is such an amazing example of following God and being faithful. A look at his life reveals just what God can do when we align ourselves with his purpose. I will set up the story here, but please read these verses as though you'd never heard them.

The Philistines and the Israelites have been at odds for a long time, and now a battle is imminent. The Philistines have disarmed the Israelites, overrun their land, and diverted their attention with raiders who deplete their supplies and repeatedly harass the people with guerrilla warfare tactics. In addition, to strip Israel of its weapons, the Philistines have made sure that Israel has no blacksmiths so that new weapons cannot be forged.

> On the day of the battle there was neither sword nor spear found
> in the hand of any of the people with Saul and Jonathan, but Saul
> and Jonathan his son had them. (1 Samuel 13:22)

Saul and Jonathan are leading an army that is ill equipped to face the enemy. There are only two swords among six hundred men. With his sword in hand, Saul remains on the outskirts and retreats to a cave, while Jonathan and his armorbearer slip away and journey to the fringe of the enemy camp.

Jonathan said to the young man who carried his armor, "Come,
let us go over to the garrison of these uncircumcised. It may be
that the LORD will work for us, for nothing can hinder the LORD
from saving by many or by few." And his armor-bearer said to
him, "Do all that is in your heart. Do as you wish. Behold, I am
with you heart and soul." (1 Samuel 14:6–7)

Do you hear Jonathan's bold stance? He knows it is not about him
or his sword. The fact that his armorbearer has no equipment will have
no sway on this battle. The outcome rests in the Lord's ability. Jonathan
knows that *nothing* can hinder the God who saves. The armorbearer
must sense faith in Jonathan's words, because he answers so decisively.
"Hey, Jonathan, do more than what you've even spoken. Do all that stirs
in your heart, all that you might dare to dream. I am not just with you
because I am present… I am with you heart and soul!"

Suddenly there is light in their eyes and vigor in their stance. Something powerful happens when two warriors agree and boldly declare
God's faithfulness and their commitment to a cause. Jonathan knows it
is full speed ahead, but he also knows he needs a strategy. Jonathan pro-
poses a scheme, then allows God to choose the outcome. It goes something like this: *God, we are going to move out of hiding and show the enemy
our position. If they chase us down, we will run. But if they invite us to come
to them, then we know you've got it covered.*

As planned, they show themselves, and the Philistine soldiers invite
them into their camp for a beating. But the enemy's invitation to a
thrashing is actually God's invitation to a victory for Israel. Without a
moment's hesitation Jonathan and his companion snap into action!

Jonathan said to his armor-bearer, "Come up after me, for the
LORD has given them into the hand of Israel." Then Jonathan

climbed up on his hands and feet, and his armor-bearer after him. And they fell before Jonathan, and his armor-bearer killed them after him. And that first strike, which Jonathan and his armor-bearer made, killed about twenty men.… And there was a panic in the camp, in the field, and among all the people. The garrison and even the raiders trembled, *the earth quaked,* and it became a very great panic. (verses 12–15, emphasis added)

What do you know? The enemy panics when two warriors take action! There is something about decisive moves forward that paralyzes the enemy. He is always routed when his attempts to intimidate are thwarted.

The soldiers who were bragging a few moments earlier tremble in terror as the very earth shakes at the approach of Jonathan and his armorbearer.

Is it not time today that we give God some options and come out of hiding?

But let us rewind a moment. What if Jonathan had not left his father's camp and made his way to the Philistines' outpost? What if he'd never spoken bold words of faith and laid out a proposition before God? Perhaps he and his armorbearer would have climbed only high enough to count the men rather than to confront the enemy. Then they would have lowered themselves, done the math, and known they were outnumbered more than ten to one. This realization would have had them sneaking back to camp. But there is no need to number the enemy when you have a revelation of who fights with you! Instead of returning to camp to file a report, Jonathan and his armorbearer pressed ahead and made history.

There is an important point here I don't want you to miss: *daughters of soldiers* can become warriors. I don't care if you come from a long line of soldiers; the spirit of a warrior resides within you! Like Jonathan, you must realize you are not limited to *what is.* Lift your eyes and open your heart to all that might be. Then you will discern more than your circumstances; you will glimpse *what God wants to do.*

When you are brave enough to leave behind what is not working (for example, cave camping), you'll find victory in some very unexpected places (the enemy's camp). It's time to take a risk and find another way.

Warriors never imagine they've been hired to do a job, because they know they are called to change their world.

Hear the Call

According to historical patterns, we walk the earth in a unique season when a hero generation is emerging in the company of mothers and fathers who wish it well. I can see the earth's economic, cultural, moral, religious, and environmental climate pressing upon you like a womb in labor. Don't allow the surrounding pressure to depress or oppress you. Don't allow the enemy to cause you to imagine it is an invitation to a beating. The pressure from all sides is part of a divine plan to mold and fashion you into someone with substance and depth. You will come out of this womb of tempering drawing a breath of strength.

> I will say to the north, "Give them up!"
>   and to the south, "Do not hold them back."
> Bring my sons from afar
>   and my daughters from the ends of the earth—
> everyone who is called by my name,
>   whom I created for my glory,
>   whom I formed and made. (Isaiah 43:6–7, NIV)

God is in the process of forming and making a people for his glory. Pressure can change our name from soldier to warrior and from servant to daughter. It is part of our tempering process. Outward pressure is always an opportunity to be inwardly transformed. And when he looks and sees that we are ready, he releases the winds and calls us forth by his name.

Warriors have learned how to trust the whispered call deep within, while soldiers feel pressured to respond to the noise that surrounds them. Soldiers and warriors process pressure in different manners. Soldiers will adopt an endure-or-escape approach. They do things to relieve the pressure: eat, drink, run, raid or pillage, shop—anything to take the mind off the conflict. It is the very reason that soldiers under constant and cruel pressure retaliate with cruelty. What they are under works its way into them and gains expression.

> *God does not give us overcoming life;*
> *He gives us life as we overcome.*
> —Oswald Chambers

Warriors respond by allowing the pressures around them to increase the pressure level within them until there is balance. They are always thinking of ways to counterattack or dismantle the enemy's ploys.

Warriors are seasoned by the battles of life, while soldiers fight for just a season in life. I understand it is better to be a soldier for a season than a coward for a lifetime, but cowardice is not even an option for a warrior-daughter.

A Tale of Two Kings

Just as we have contrasted the lives of warriors and soldiers, let us now compare two warring kings—Israel's first king, Saul, and her final and forever King, Jesus.

Israel's soldier-king, Saul, was anointed as both king and deliverer because Israel wanted to be like the other nations. They wanted a king to call their own—a figurehead of sorts that they could point to with pride.

Rather than submitting to the invisible, invincible, eternal God Most High, they wanted someone they could see and touch. They wanted a human champion who could lead them into battle rather than a heavenly King who would fight for them. God answered their request with an extraordinary young man named Saul:

> And when he stood among the people, he was taller than any
> of the people from his shoulders upward. And Samuel said to all
> the people, "Do you see him whom the LORD has chosen? *There
> is none like him among all the people.*" And all the people shouted,
> "Long live the king!" (1 Samuel 10:23–24, emphasis added)

Saul was a standout among his people—he towered over them. But not only was he strong; he was very good looking.

God established Saul's reign with an explosive display of deliverance power. Sadly, it wasn't long after this show of strength that Saul made a fatal mistake. Samuel instructed Saul to meet the Philistines in battle, but he was to wait and was not to engage this enemy until Samuel made the appropriate prebattle sacrifices on Israel's behalf. Saul had gathered his small army in Gilgal in preparation to meet Philistine forces so vast they could not be numbered.

As Saul waited, the enemy army increased in number. Terrified, Saul's men deserted their posts and fled across the river in droves until only six hundred remained. Instead of lifting his eyes to get God's warrior perspective (I believe God had all the Philistines show up so Saul could take them all out!), Saul allowed these circumstances to overwhelm him, and he decided to take matters into his own hands. Rather than encourage his men and remind them that God could save by many or by few, he allowed their fear to incite him to disobedience:

> Saul said to Samuel, *"I have sinned, for I have transgressed the commandment of the LORD and your words, because I feared the people and obeyed their voice."* (15:24, emphasis added)

You will ultimately serve and obey what you fear. God had placed Saul head and shoulders above the people so they could look up to him, but instead he stooped to their level. Saul suffered and lost his kingdom due to repeated acts of disobedience. Sadly, Saul was an insecure leader who measured his worth by what the people said about him.

Saul's downward slide began with disobedience and culminated in periods of dark and oppressive depression caused by a destructive and at times violent spirit. Saul died as he had lived, afraid of what others might do to him.

Wounded by arrows and surrounded by the enemy's army, Saul responded by taking matters into his own hands. In order to avoid the torment of his enemies, the frightened king took his own life by falling upon an upturned sword braced against the ground. The sword on Saul's hip was drawn in response to fear. The only fear a king should dare to harbor is the fear of the Lord.

> Then Saul said to his armor-bearer, "Draw your sword and thrust me through with it, *lest these uncircumcised come and mistreat me."* But his armor-bearer would not, for he feared greatly. Therefore Saul took his own sword and fell upon it. (1 Chronicles 10:4, emphasis added)

When the armorbearer refused, Saul took his own life. Is there any act that declares hopelessness with greater finality than suicide? When the armies of Israel heard that their king and his sons were dead, they likewise lost every remnant of hope and abandoned their cities, and the enemy took possession of Israel's homes and lands.

In contrast Jesus learned obedience through what he suffered, and it won him a kingdom:

> Even though Jesus was God's Son, *he learned obedience from the things he suffered.* In this way, God qualified him as a perfect High Priest, and he became the source of eternal salvation for all those who obey him. (Hebrews 5:8–9, NLT, emphasis added)

Let's contrast how these warrior-kings faced both their cruel enemies and death.

Saul took matters into his own hands to avoid the mistreatment of his enemies. Jesus removed his hands from the situation and presented himself to his enemies, knowing what they would do to him.

Saul fell upon his sword to avoid suffering. Jesus stretched himself upon the cross to take away ours.

Saul's suicide cheated his enemies. Jesus's sacrifice cheated death.

Whom would you rather cheat? Which is greater—to experience victory over your enemies or to realize triumph over the enemy of all?

In death the soldier-king Saul exposed his people to loss by abandoning them. In death Jesus restored all that was lost and adopted us as his own. Our Warrior-King Jesus did all this for us even when he was disowned by us. Saul lived for the acknowledgment of his people. Jesus died so God would acknowledge us.

King Jesus was fathered by God, baptized by John, filled with the Holy Spirit, and rejected by his own. Jesus surrendered himself to the brutality of his enemies. He allowed them to mock him and make violent sport of him as they beat him beyond recognition. He endured interrogations, false witnesses, and the public humiliation of a trial in which he was condemned to death by the very people he came to raise to life.

Yet through all this he remained silent. Jesus did not carry a sword of metal on his hip. His very words were a two-edged sword of the Spirit, which he kept sheathed out of love. King Jesus did all this for those who disowned him.

By examining the Cross through the lens of a warrior, I learned *there is no greater weapon than a life laid down.*

Our Savior was not on a suicide mission. He was not a religious zealot with a bomb strapped on his back, seeing how many lives he could steal through his death. He didn't die to escape earthly suffering or cheat a cruel enemy. Jesus was a defenseless, silent lamb who cheated the roaring leviathan of death.

No one took the life of Jesus. He gave it and, by dying, rescued our lives. He refused deliverance and relief so he could be both to us.

Fencing Fact

The road to fencing is twofold. First, exercise patience. Second, practice.

Our Warrior-King prayed as his enemies approached. Rather than fight, Jesus surrendered to their cruelty. Rather than take matters into his hands and fall upon the sword Peter carried, he carried the cross. And when Jesus reached the hill on which he was destined to die, he lay down upon the sword of the cross and allowed his hands to be nailed "to the hilt." Then the Roman soldiers lifted the unbearable wooden sword and planted its cruel point like a murderous tree root in the ground.

When he sees all that is accomplished by his anguish,
    he will be satisfied.

And because of his experience,
    my righteous servant will make it possible
for many to be counted righteous,
    for he will bear all their sins.
I will give him the *honors of a victorious soldier,*
    because he exposed himself to death. (Isaiah 53:11–12, NLT,
        emphasis added)

The fact that Jesus exposed himself to death means that he could have hidden from it. Isaiah declares the why behind the Cross. Jesus understood the only way to win was to surrender to the highest power (his Father's will), and you and I were the prize. Jesus endured agony and shame so that his victory might be revealed in us. Through his anguish we experienced righteousness. We are his triumphant accomplishment.

●   ●   ●

God will always send us the grace and strength we need to do his will. Warriors obey their commander, and when they fail (as all do), they don't blame others. Jesus took our blame and followed his Father's will.

Lovely One, you are the daughter of a triumphant Warrior-King. The warrior's sword you carry represents honor, virtue, courage, beauty, loyalty, and freedom from fear. In the next section we will learn how to wield these with purpose.

No normal, healthy saint ever chooses suffering;
he simply chooses God's will, just as Jesus did,
whether it means suffering or not.
—OSWALD CHAMBERS

7

Forging a Sword

Hard times don't create heroes. It is during the hard times when the "hero" within us is revealed.

—Bob Riley

The process of making a sword is a whole lot like the process of making a life.

Fire, water, and pressure are the tools used to refine metal, temper steel, and create swords. In the process of forging a sword, pressure is usually applied immediately after heating. Pressure works best when the subject is pliable, because that which is brittle will break! With the forging of a sword, there is repeated hammering.

My favorite story about the making of a sword is found in Stephen Lawhead's epic *The Warlords of Nin*. A dark and cruel enemy has invaded the land, and to combat this ruthless nemesis, a sword of light is required. There is no way to do justice to the process described in Lawhead's book, but suffice it to say the core of the sword is fashioned by taking separate pieces of metal, such as steel, and working them into a unified whole. The process of sword making is not altogether different from that of weaving. Once heated, that which is stiff becomes pliable enough to braid and twist, thus creating a tension that fuses the separate strands into a whole.

Then the woven metal visits the crucible of fire to be heated. After that it is cooled and hammered and stretched yet again. This dance between extremes is a process known as tempering.

Next there is hammering, shaping, and polishing before a blade appears and is ready to be attached to a hilt, which also has been processed and tempered in order for it to be handled.

Likewise, God uses the elements of fire, water, and pressure to refine his daughters in order to transform our weaknesses into strengths, our rigidity into flexibility. He hones a shapeless life into one of sharp and focused purpose.

Water

Water is a compound of contradictions. I just glanced out my hotel window, and in my limited range of view, I see children laughing and playing in the calm, clear shallows of the Pacific Ocean. At the same time farther out on the horizon, I see dark waves crashing—the evidence of a treacherous riptide. You have to love our amazing God, who created water as a unique medium we can play in, but at the same time it has the potential to kill us.

Water has the power to refresh or overwhelm. It can gently lift us to the surface on a float or drive us tumbling into its depths. You can't live long without it or long within it. Water has the power to gently wash and irrigate fields or wipe out cities with a tsunami wave.

Fire

Then there is the element of fire. It invites us closer with a promise of warmth, but come too close and it will burn. Controlled fires refine, but uncontrolled wildfires consume. Fire can safely light the way or leave a trail of destruction and ashes in its wake. Fire is at once humanity's friend and enemy, a force of nature to be harnessed but never toyed with.

The ability to make and contain fire is one of the talents that set humans apart from the animal kingdom. Over the millenniums we have learned to intensify the temperature of the flame so that shapes can shift. Under intense heat solids become liquids, and we have learned to heat forges to as high as 3,272 degrees Fahrenheit in order to combine iron with other alloys and make something as sturdy and solid as steel. This merging of matter yields metals that have the best properties of both. Once they are blended so there is no separation, they are cooled back to a solid that can be shaped as its heated hue shifts from fiery white to orange and finally to dull gray.

We see this transformation in the blowing of glass and the creation of crystal. Magnificent vessels with the ability to contain water are created from the fusing of particles as miniscule and disjointed as shifting sand.

Water and fire are also tangible elements that take on multiple forms in our spiritual walk.

> *Fear not,* for I have redeemed you;
>   I have called you by name, you are mine.
> *When you pass through the waters, I will be with you;*
>   and through the rivers, they shall not overwhelm you;
> *when you walk through fire* you shall not be burned,
>   *and the flame shall not consume you.* (Isaiah 43:1–2,
>   emphasis added)

Notice that even before water and fire are introduced, the issue of fear is addressed. We have no reason to fear, because not only has our Father redeemed us, but we have been individually named and adopted as God's own. It is important to note Isaiah's choice of terms in these verses. This dynamic of passing through water and fire is not referred to as an "if" possibility but is clearly tagged as a "when" occurrence.

Sometimes I think it is actually more reassuring in this context. If the promise were attached to "*if* you pass through waters, rivers, fire, or flame," I could run the risk of being caught off guard. Human nature will go to great lengths to avoid *if* passageways. As Isaiah penned it here, we know ahead of time that the water and fire courses of life are unavoidable and not necessarily the result of mistakes on our part.

In addition to the assurance that there will be waters and rivers, fires and flames, it appears these types of experiences will happen multiple times. The good news is that you're just passing through. Don't give in to the inclination to murmur and complain, because neither fire nor water is a friendly place to camp. They are processes to successfully navigate.

Throughout the Bible we see God repeatedly use bodies of water as a symbol of transition. The children of Israel left behind their years of Egyptian bondage in the depths of the Red Sea and then left their years of desert wandering at the banks of the Jordan River before entering their season of promise.

Fire also represents a declaration of covenant. God provided the fire when he first made a covenant with Abraham. Later when Israel had strayed and listened to false prophets, God answered with fire as Elijah called Israel to repentance. The fiery furnace became a haven for the children of Israel who refused to bow to Nebuchadnezzar's idol, yet the fire consumed those who had bowed to the idol.

Chances are you have already journeyed through a bit of water and fire. This may have happened when you were unaware that water was present. We each pass through waters so gentle, temperate, and thorough that they wash away our sins even though we are physically unaware. There is a moment of immersion in water as we bury our old lives and rise up renewed, as in the sacrament of baptism. Then there are raging rivers we must cross that frighten us as they threaten to overwhelm us, such as when we go through hard times.

Life begins in water, and water sustains life. God the Father began the creation process as his Spirit hovered over the face of the waters. Likewise, our lives begin in a sea within our mothers' wombs. Water is the universal solvent that's ultimate purpose is to wash. But water does more than cleanse; it lifts. Water can support what is too heavy to bear on land and transport ships down rivers and across oceans to lands far away.

We speak of fire and water here because they are very much a part of forging the mettle of our lives, just as they are part of the tempering of a sword. As we discuss the forging of a sword, we will realize it happens first in the processing of the one who bears it. In ancient cultures, ranging from the times of the samurai to the medieval knights, before men were granted the honor of wielding a sword, they were first subjected to a code of ethics.

> *For in the end, freedom is a personal and lonely battle;*
> *and one faces down fears of today so that those*
> *of tomorrow might be engaged.*
> —ALICE WALKER

I found it humorous that in order to temper the fierceness of individual samurai, these warriors were encouraged to balance their aggressive nature by mastering the normally feminine arts of flower arranging and the tea ceremony. Likewise, I don't think it is too much of a stretch for us women to add a bit of combat arts and etiquette to our lives.

> *Behold, I have refined you, but not as silver;*
> *I have tried you in the furnace of affliction.*

For my own sake, for my own sake, I do it,
  for how should my name be profaned?
  My glory I will not give to another. (Isaiah 48:10–11,
         emphasis added)

The charge to "behold" is an invitation to look at something from a vaster vantage. Opening this verse with *behold* clues us in to the fact that the people going through the process probably had no idea they were being refined. They just thought they were going through that four-letter special name for the underworld!

God gives us a new view from his eternal vantage point. He is the ultimate refiner of our lives. Remember, refinement is a good thing. But good does not always mean pain- and trouble-free. For example, giving birth is a good thing, but I never found it to be pain-free. This life is full of furnaces called affliction. The key to successfully navigating them is knowing that our God is in charge of setting both the temperature and the timer.

Before we go any further, let's define this word *affliction.* In the context of Bible definitions, it most commonly means suffering under physical and/or mental distress, difficulties, burdens, problems, pain, trouble, misery, misfortune, and hardship. There are a few references to illness, but the majority of times it appears to be when God's people experience a smackdown of epic proportions.

There's more to come: We continue to shout our praise even when we're hemmed in with troubles, because we know how troubles can develop passionate patience in us, and how that patience in turn *forges the tempered steel of virtue,* keeping us alert for whatever God will do next. In alert expectancy such as this, we're never left feeling shortchanged. (Romans 5:3–5, MSG, emphasis added)

So let's bring this close to home. Recently I took a poll on Facebook and asked people to list their three most challenging issues or areas of affliction at the present time. Here were the top three:

1. *Relationship challenges* with spouse, siblings, children, leaders, or friends. There were both the lonely married and the lonely unmarried.

2. *Financial challenges* resulting from unemployment, credit card and other debt due to unwise purchases, or health issues.

3. *Challenges in finding life purpose* and the daily discipline to pursue what is in their hearts.

Let's be honest…affliction is no fun. My heart went out to people as I read their responses. There are two types of afflictions we all go through—troubles that are self-inflicted and trials that are God backed. I don't believe God always causes our problems, but he uses them as an opportunity to refine us for his glory. In both cases the solution is the same: turn to him! He is our source, and his Word is both his will and our weapon of promise.

There is a reason why the phrase "light a fire under you" has poignant meaning: when things get uncomfortable, you are willing to move!

> *This is as true in everyday life as it is in battle:*
> *we are given one life and the decision is ours whether*
> *to wait for circumstances to make up our mind,*
> *or whether to act, and in acting, to live.*
> —GENERAL OMAR N. BRADLEY

Lessons that are learned through hardship always become the most valuable because they are often the most personal.

Pressure

Then pressure is added to the dynamic of fire and water.

To explore what this process of tempering might look like from the vantage of the Scriptures, I am going to draw on some of my least favorite Bible verses, found in the book of James.

The English Standard Version invites us to "count it all joy, *my brothers,* when you meet trials of various kinds" (1:2, emphasis added). Well, I think you already know that trials are not gender specific. But just so the girls feel included in this admonition, I am going to add the corresponding verse from The Message: "Consider it a sheer gift, *friends,* when tests and challenges come at you from all sides" (verse 2, emphasis added).

Can James be serious? Is he honestly telling us to number trials as *pure joy* and to consider the tests and challenges that press upon us from every direction as *gifts?* Imagine calling your best friend on the worst day of your life, and after you tearfully tell her the specifics of unexpected trials on every front, she enthusiastically exclaims, "What a gift! Let's celebrate. You, my friend, are surrounded!"

You might very well hang up on her and call another friend who will at least say that she is sorry your day was so awful and that she will pray that tomorrow is better. This is perhaps where the clash between our human perspective and heaven's vantage is the most evident. Our God loves triumphing over what looks impossible; therefore, he calls an ambush without any means of escape "an opportunity"! After all, James was the brother of Jesus. So he must have had some insight we lack, because he goes on to say, "For you know that the testing of your faith produces steadfastness" (verse 3).

The Message describes the process this way: "You know that under pressure, your faith-life is forced into the open and shows its true colors."

Okay, truth time. I know that under pressure my faith has been forced out into the open, and at times I have not liked what I have seen. The weight of life circumstances bore down upon me, and I suddenly appeared in colors that were less than flattering. Not only was the color all wrong, but *steadfast* would not have been the word to describe my response.

I don't think God meant for trials to cause guys to win and girls to whine, so I knew it was time for me to buck up.

The dynamic of trials causes the invisible to become visible. Under pressure, things appear that remain hidden in the absence of difficulty. God wants us to thrive whether we are under pressure or free floating.

Life is not like a visit to the massage therapist, where you get to choose the level of intensity you enjoy. When hardship strikes, no one asks if you would like your pressure light, medium, or deep. Tempered daughters of God are resilient. We have the capacity to flourish under all types of trials in every season.

I live in Colorado, where winters are long and springs are nearly nonexistent. Under normal weather patterns we may have a blizzard, then sudden summer. If I want to have certain types of flowers bloom under these conditions, I have to alter the conditions. I create an artificially mild winter by putting the bulbs in a refrigerator drawer. I follow this up with a false spring, which occurs in the safety of my laundry room window, and—*boom*—my flowers are tricked into blooming out of season. I think God likes to do much the same thing but by way of a very different process: trials and pressure are what cause us to bloom or bust.

Fencing Fact

Weakness can give the appearance of strength in fencing, and strength, weakness.

James continues to extol the virtue of enduring trials in the next verse: "And let steadfastness have its full effect, that you may be perfect and complete, lacking in nothing" (verse 4).

For those of us who need to hear this verse in a bit clearer language, there is The Message's version: "So don't try to get out of anything prematurely. Let it do its work so you become mature and well-developed, not deficient in any way" (verses 3–4).

We all go through tests, so why not allow them to have a full effect? I have learned that if I pull out of something too early, it usually means a retest in the future. They say that when you are working a muscle group, the growth happens when you push yourself to the point of muscle failure. When you give all you can give, then somehow you pull from a God source outside yourself and give just a bit more—one more kind word, caring touch, forgiving word, prayer lifted, call made. In other words, being consistent during a trial tempers our faith so that it reaches full maturity.

This approach requires heavenly wisdom, so James adds verse 5: "If any of you lacks wisdom, let him ask God, who gives generously to all without reproach, and it will be given him." And The Message echoes: "If you don't know what you're doing, pray to the Father. He loves to help. You'll get his help, and won't be condescended to when you ask for it."

God is our source of wisdom. He is generous rather than stingy with his counsel. I believe he strategically positions us so that we have to ask for his help. He is not in heaven uninvolved, with his arms crossed, saying to Jesus, "Can you believe this? They still can't figure this out." No, he loves it when we involve him! As God has fast-tracked my life, I find that I often wake up not even knowing where I am, not to mention what I am doing! I say, *Heavenly Father, today I need your wisdom.* And he answers, *Daughter, I have got you covered.* But it seems there is an even more specific way God likes to hear these prayers composed.

But *let him [her] ask in faith, with no doubting,* for the one who
doubts is like a wave of the sea that is driven and tossed by the

wind. For that person must not suppose that [she] will receive anything from the Lord; he [she] is a double-minded man [woman], unstable in all his [her] ways. (verses 6–8)

Ask boldly, believingly, without a second thought. People who "worry their prayers" are like wind-whipped waves. Don't think you're going to get anything from the Master that way, adrift at sea, keeping all your options open. (verses 6–8, MSG)

God loves when we pray boldly without a shadow of a doubt. I like to think of it this way: God invites us to pray in such a way that it scares what is scared within us! In the last few years, God has stretched John and me and all the staff of Messenger International. We have had no choice but to join hearts and hands and pray prayers that astounded our ears and caused our hearts to leap as they left our mouths.

> God loves when we pray boldly without a shadow of a doubt.

One such scenario was when John shared with our lead team that he really sensed God challenging us to give away 250,000 books in the course of one calendar year.

I threw up in my mouth! The most we'd given away before was 70,000 books in one year. Two hundred and fifty thousand seemed too big a leap to make. So I offered a second thought.

"How about we start by giving away 100,000?"

It was not my best moment.

John responded very quickly before my doubt could fill the room.

"Lisa, my faith is attached to 250,000 books."

Well, there we had it. We all stood and prayed a prayer that sounded impossibly outlandish at the time. But in all honesty, if you are not praying the type of prayers that scare you, your prayers are certainly not frightening our enemy. But apparently our bold request was just what heaven was waiting to hear. Within days a plan began to unfold, and the resources to undertake the project were revealed. Churches, friends, and even a rock star partnered with us in the endeavor to see the messages we steward travel free of charge to various nations. Books were translated into Arabic, Farsi, Armenian, Urdu, Chinese, Vietnamese, Khmer, Bulgarian, Indonesian, and many more languages. Books in languages I don't even know how to spell found their way into the hands of isolated leaders and brothers and sisters.

Swords may be double edged but never double minded. If we choose to strike, we must strike true.

> *The battle of life is, in most cases, fought uphill; and*
> *to win it without a struggle were perhaps to win it*
> *without honor. If there were no difficulties, there would*
> *be no success; if there were nothing to struggle for,*
> *there would be nothing to be achieved.*
> —SAMUEL SMILES

So, Lovely One, it is up to you. You can run and hide, curse and cry in an attempt to escape the hardships of life and in the process be overcome. Or you can choose to allow adversity to be a crucible in your life that tempers your strength.

It is clear to us, friends, that *God not only loves you very much but also has put his hand on you for something special.* When the Message we preached came to you, it wasn't just words. Something happened in you. The Holy Spirit put steel in your convictions. (1 Thessalonians 1:5, MSG, emphasis added)

As this chapter closes, here is my prayer for you.

Dear Heavenly Father,

May we, your daughters, be one with your heart and heaven's purpose. May our very lives be an intricately woven expression of all that you long for us to live, touch, see, hear, and have. Make us one. We submit to your process. Have your way in the fiery forge and in the baptism of water. Shape us into something so fierce and flexible that every facet of our lives would declare your love and power to save. In Jesus's name, amen.

In the next section we will learn how to wield these with purpose.

PART THREE

ARMED

8

Sword Words

For though we walk in the flesh, we are not waging
war according to the flesh. For the weapons
of our warfare are not of the flesh but have divine
power to destroy strongholds.

—2 Corinthians 10:3-4

The saber we've been entrusted to bear is not lifted with our hands; it is raised by our words. We speak the Word of God as a weapon heard long before it is ever seen. The last time the world saw the sword, or Word of God, in its mightiest form was when Jesus walked our earth. He longs for us to grow collectively into this stature.

Like our Savior Lord, we have the power to draw forth our sword by the words we choose to speak. We speak as ambassadors of faith, hope, and his love so that the people of earth will know they have been reconciled to the God of all through the death of his Son. We are ministers of hope whose words are seasoned with salt and light and sound foreign in a world peppered with darkness. Words are invisible, but if misused, they can prove deadly.

Words are potent weapons for all causes, good or bad.
—Manly P. Hall

We have the power to speak words that can open or close hearts. Now is the time to speak heaven's words with the intention of releasing others by our words and deeds.

Our ancient language unites all that was once divided because it is the very words of God. Think of it: God has given us his language, and we don't have to learn heaven's grammar or punctuation to use it. He has framed the words in strength and carefully structured each sentence so that every syllable is woven with power and punctuated by promise.

> All Scripture is inspired by God and is useful to teach us what is
> true and to make us realize what is wrong in our lives. It corrects
> us when we are wrong and teaches us to do what is right. God
> uses it to prepare and equip his people to do every good work.
> (2 Timothy 3:16–17, NLT)

Notice it doesn't say some scriptures are inspired and useful, but all Scripture teaches, corrects, prepares, and equips. If we pick and choose what we speak forth and live out, we will find ourselves ill equipped and unprepared for what awaits us in the future. The Scriptures become our mirror. God's Word has the power to change us so that we reflect what is true and deflect what is false. Beholding the Word causes us to change not only the way we speak but the very origins of our words.

> He who comes from above is above all. He who is of the earth
> belongs to the earth and speaks in an earthly way. (John 3:31)

Language has the power to elevate or demean, bless or curse, heal or wound. We can speak after the manner of this earth or after the pattern of heaven. The Message paraphrases John 3:31 this way:

The One who comes from above is head and shoulders over other messengers from God. The earthborn is earthbound and speaks earth language; the heavenborn is in a league of his own.

We are the earthborn, reborn for heaven. If I discovered I would live out the rest of my days on earth in Italy, it would make sense to learn Italian. Well, we will live out eternity in heaven, so it makes sense to learn heaven's language now. It is time we speak the language of our rebirth, of our Father's land.

> My heart is stirred by a noble theme
> > as I recite my verses for the king;
> > my tongue is the pen of a skillful writer. (Psalm 45:1, NIV)

God wants to display his power in and through you. He never meant for us to live our lives limited to the language and therefore the realm of human power. Prayer invites us to experience a divine intervention that raises us to a new vantage that is head and shoulders above the limits of our human language. Our new height gives us newfound perspective. We lift swords when we lift his Word: "Death and life are in the power of the tongue" (Proverbs 18:21).

We will live out eternity in heaven, so it makes sense to learn heaven's language now.

God's words are flawless and vibrant. They are likened to our living swords that light the darkness. He has entrusted his children with a powerful, holy, ancient language. These living words should be used honorably. When his holy words are misused or wielded in angry judgment, the reflection is twisted, and heaven's light is marred by darkness.

I would love to speak a foreign language. It would be so amazing to have a working grasp of words that could welcome me into another country. Like most Americans, I took the required two years of a foreign language, but without anyone to converse with, my limited mastery of French quickly fell away. If only they'd offered Italian, my story would now be different. Though my father was born in the United States, his first language was not English. His mother and father were born on the island of Sicily and therefore spoke Italian. In those days Italians were thought of as ignorant, poor immigrants. Their language connected them with the Italian community but isolated them from English-speaking Americans. My father quickly learned that his accent made him stand out at school, and it is hard to lose an accent when you speak one language at home and a different one each day at school. My grandmother was widowed when my father was only ten. As the oldest son, he worked hard to teach his mother English so she could support the family.

As my father used to tell it, he ran away at a young age, changed his name from Venerando to Joseph, served in the navy, and played football at Indiana University. After college he worked for an airline, married my mother, who was a flight attendant, and strived hard to distance himself from any connection with the poverty of his upbringing.

The decades passed, and my father became a successful business-man. I grew up being called a WOP (without papers), but I actually had no idea what my Indiana counterparts were talking about. All I knew was that when we gathered with my father's family at my grandmother's house, the brothers spoke to one another in passionate and loud tones in a musical language I never heard in my home. Sadly, only a few phrases and songs were passed on to me. I wish I had known to ask for more. Even now when I travel to Italy, I find myself remembering the rhythms of my grandmother's speech. It is as though my father's mother tongue calls to his daughter.

Do you long to speak a foreign language? Please don't think I'm referring to the tedious labor of learning its grammar. I mean having an actual, innate understanding so deep you could speak it from your heart.

Perhaps you are already fluent in a foreign language. If so, then I don't have to tell you how this ability opens doors and makes immediate connections between strangers from different worlds. The heady combination of shared language and purpose connects the inhabitants of different countries in powerful ways.

When we translated our books into various foreign languages, we were awed by the way these messages found their way into the hands of others. The formerly isolated felt included, and the recipients felt their need had been dignified by the intentional gift of others. Not only did they receive the Word of God in their language, but they received it within the framework of shared human experiences so they could apply it to their daily world.

When I wrote the book *Nurture*, I framed this attribute as a language of the heart that women hold in common. Like language, nurture expresses itself in both verbal and nonverbal ways. It is an example of our common mother tongue as surely as the native language expresses the national origin of our birth.

As important as both of these are, with this book I hope to unearth another layer. I want to delve a bit deeper and speak of a language even more powerful than the language of our native origins or our heart's mother tongue.

This framework of language has the power to move beyond the connection of people. The very words of it are woven with the substantive power to move the unseen into the seen and create something out of nothing.

When our Father spoke, creation was set in motion. Out of a dark void of shapeless chaos, order and light burst forth. If we are going to

be awed daughters who do awe-inspiring things to honor our awesome
God, we need his words and name.

As with our Father, our thoughts are released when we speak. God
created us with an intimate understanding of what it is to receive, carry,
and, in the fullness of time, birth life. "Out of the abundance of the heart
the mouth speaks" (Matthew 12:34). We usually hear this referenced as
an admonition to guard our hearts or to take stock of what is stored up in
our hearts by listening to what comes out of our mouths. But this time I
want to look at the scripture through a different lens, because out of the
abundance of God's heart, he spoke the universe of galaxies into existence.

> For his invisible attributes, namely, his eternal power and divine
> nature, have been clearly perceived, ever since the creation of the
> world, in the things that have been made. (Romans 1:20)

You are even more exciting and complex than oceans, mountains,
and lions! You, Lovely One, reflect an attribute of our invisible God.

When this language is whispered, vast distances are instantaneously
spanned, and the realms of earth and heaven are unified. And it is ours to
speak because it is the language of our Father.

Fencing Fact

Timing and blocking actions neutralize the attacking force of even the most aggressive fencer.

In addition to being a collection of written God words that form swords, the Holy
Scriptures are the living, breathing language
of our true home. And as such, each sentence is filled with imagery and instructions
for both our earth journey now and that high
and holy place.

His Word supersedes all that we've ever known
as language, because his words were the genesis of all we now see. Our
Father's language can be flawlessly spoken by everyone, regardless of a

person's native tongue and accent. These powerful and ancient texts are available to every tribe and dialect.

The dynamic of foreign languages was birthed when God scattered a disobedient people who all shared a common language. The following is the account of the Tower of Babel.

> The LORD came down to see the city and the tower, which the children of man had built. And the LORD said, "Behold, they are one people, and they have all one language, and this is only the beginning of what they will do. And nothing that they propose to do will now be impossible for them. Come, let us go down and there confuse their language, so that they may not understand one another's speech." So the LORD dispersed them from there over the face of all the earth, and they left off building the city. Therefore its name was called Babel, because there the LORD confused the language of all the earth. And from there the LORD dispersed them over the face of all the earth. (Genesis 11:5–9)

It is interesting to note that this construction project of the seemingly *impossible* would have been *possible* because of two factors: a united people and a shared language. Their endeavor would have been successful even though it was not God authored. Their plans were motivated by outright disobedience to God's directive in Genesis 1. The confusion of languages not only *stopped* their progress, but it *scattered* a unified people to the four corners of the earth. The story of our human existence began with one language, and I believe it will end with one language…the language of the wonder of God.

> At this sound the multitude came together, and they were bewildered, because each one was hearing them speak in his own

language. And they were amazed and astonished, saying, "Are not all these who are speaking Galileans? And how is it that we hear, each of us in his own native language? Parthians and Medes and Elamites and residents of Mesopotamia, Judea and Cappadocia, Pontus and Asia, Phrygia and Pamphylia, Egypt and the parts of Libya belonging to Cyrene, and visitors from Rome, both Jews and proselytes, Cretans and Arabians—*we hear them telling in our own tongues the mighty works of God.*" (Acts 2:6–11, emphasis added)

Multitudes gather when heaven finds voice on earth. When we truly have something to say, God finds a way to interpret it for all who need to hear. When we yield ourselves to speak his words by the power of his Spirit, astonishing things can happen. I so long for this unified expression of God's wonder.

Don't you love the fact that God chose people from a region that was considered to be illiterate (Galilee) to declare his glorious wonders to the devout and well educated who had gathered in Jerusalem from every area? No one was left out. Even more important than sharing a common earthly language that sounds the same is the collective power of saying the same thing. On the Day of Pentecost, the declarations of heaven invaded earth, and all who were present knew it.

Our God Most High is triumphant. His glorious love and wondrous mercy know no bounds. The gift of salvation is through faith in him alone, and all who seek him find grace and hope.

The point here is not whether you believe in speaking in tongues. There are bigger questions to be answered: Will we choose to use our words in a way that removes us from the picture and glorifies God? Will we speak in our flawed manner or tell of his flawless works? Will we be a unified voice by allowing his Spirit to fill us?

I have never seen a commitment to unity work unless all participants were aligned with a higher cause. Unifying ourselves with our Father's purposes and language will initiate or begin anew God's plan and unify a people around his purpose.

With so many pieces of the sword (his body and his Word) disconnected and removed from our immediate sight, we've only known our part…in part! To understand the function of a part, it is best to have an idea of the image of the whole.

Missing pieces would naturally mean that there are parts we know… and other parts where the Spirit and the Word of God fill in the blanks. We prophesy and speak a word of faith to create substance for what we've yet to see of the other part. He is our all in all; we are part of a whole.

For far too long the Word has been interpreted rather than proclaimed. We have gotten into the habit of passing it through the filter of human experiences, social preferences, current prejudices, and the limited counsel of the human mind rather than simply declaring what was so powerfully and eternally spoken and recorded. We've interpreted the gospel rather than expressed it.

> **For far too long the Word has been interpreted rather than proclaimed.**

The temptation has been to interpret the Word according to the small part we play or possess rather than proclaim the Word in the mysterious form of its entirety. It takes faith to declare a language we do not understand.

> By faith we understand that the worlds have been framed by the word of God, so that what is seen hath not been made out of things which appear. (Hebrews 11:3, ASV)

God framed the world we see by words we cannot see. When we act like our Father and echo his words, the sword finds its substance. When we simply declare what was already powerfully and eternally wrought in heaven, the created earth recognizes the words and aligns itself to the will of its Creator.

Far too much is lost in interpretation when we pass the words of heaven through the filter of earth rather than fashion the earth with the words of heaven. Our wisdom is best drawn from the Ancient of Days rather than from the people of our day. Quite honestly, I always thought Job's friends sounded brilliant until God showed up!

"Who is this that *hides* counsel without knowledge?"
Therefore I have uttered what I did not understand,
   things too wonderful for me, which I did not know.
      (Job 42:3, emphasis added)

Other Bible versions use the words *obscures, muddies,* and *questions* to elaborate on this word *hides.* When we attempt to explain, or explain away, what we do not understand, we shadow or darken the light of God's counsel. We question his greatness when we dull the edges of his heavenly Word.

If I send one of my sons to tell one of his brothers, "Mom wants you downstairs immediately," I expect him to repeat it just as I said it. But communication gets muddied when he drops off something I said or adds in something I didn't. For example, "Mom wants you downstairs immediately to set the table." (Perhaps added because he wanted his brother to set the table.) If I've called him down to walk the dog or simply to spend time with him, there is going to be some confusion. Or if the message is relayed as "Mom wants you downstairs," without a time assignment, my son may say, "Okay." But without knowing the immediacy factor, he may delay his compliance. These are minor examples that can go major on a larger scale.

God is the only One who knows it all. He knows we don't know it all, which is the reason he gave us the wisdom of his ways and thoughts on just about everything that matters. But, like my sons, we often assume that the why behind his reasoning or the timing isn't important.

How does this fit with Paul's charge to his spiritual son, Timothy?

> *Preach the word;* be *urgent in season, out of season; reprove, rebuke, exhort,* with all longsuffering and teaching. For *the time will come when they will not endure the sound doctrine;* but, having itching ears, will heap to themselves teachers after their own lusts; *and will turn away* their ears *from the truth,* and turn aside unto fables. (2 Timothy 4:2–4, ASV, emphasis added)

Rather than preach *light words,* preach *words of light*! I understand there was a season in the past when the sword of God's Word was spoken without light, as it was wielded in legalism. Adding our agenda will always distort the brilliance of God's Word. When people have been hurt by what was meant to heal, they flinch under its influence.

In order not to frighten people, many ministers and leaders pulled back a bit, and in an attempt to be seeker sensitive, they added a derivative language, almost a slang form of God's Word. I think seeker-sensitive methods are great, but we make a mistake when we allow our methodology to compromise God's message.

> *Broadly speaking, the short words are best,*
> *and the old words best of all.*
> —WINSTON CHURCHILL

Winston Churchill was a brilliant communicator whose words have reached far beyond his realm and day and continue to speak to our time.

I like to think that this quote explains how short, concise words speak with clarity and the older words weather the ravages of time best. As *timely* as any human words are, they eventually become dated in the presence of the *timeless* eternal.

In Jesus's time the Jews used two languages. Hebrew was reserved for the temple and the study of the holy scripts. Aramaic was the language for everyday use in the home and marketplace. Jesus brought the sacred, hidden words and power of God to the people in the streets, homes, and marketplace. But he did not allow the sacred to be treated as common, even though he treated the common people as sacred.

In our attempts to be all things to all people, have we allowed our words to become common or profane and lessened the eternal weight of the holy? Allow me to use myself as an example. For many years now I have told audiences to leave the trappings of their past because with God "your past is not your future."

It is a phrase God gave me in 1994 while I was in prayer. It is usually what the attendees remember as a takeaway phrase. As true as it is, this saying has a shelf life or an expiration date. It has transformative power when it is declared along with the scriptures that back it. "Your past is not your future" is a condensed version of Philippians 3:13–14:

> But one thing I do: forgetting what lies behind and straining forward to what lies ahead, I press on toward the goal for the prize of the upward call of God in Christ Jesus.

What I said is *true,* but it wields less power than truth. Slang derivatives of truth lack the power of the original. We can no longer live off words that are void of power, imagining that the sacred texts aren't necessary anymore in our presentations. We will always fall short when we seek to be scriptural without scriptures.

Catch phrases are easy to remember because they are so…catchy. In this day of such interconnected social media, if a group of words is pithy enough, it can travel the globe in a span of minutes. But what does it leave in its wake? Do Facebook and Twitter have the power to transform? I certainly hope so, because many millions of people are spending a lot of time in their sphere of influence. I pray it is not creating a generation of wise fools who know everything and do nothing.

Why do we imagine the invitation to selah (be still and awed by wonder) was inserted so frequently throughout the psalms? The pauses allow time for the sacred words to pierce any shadowed thought realms with the brilliance of their timelessness. Without the voice of the Holy Spirit, there is no conviction of sin and ultimately no truly wise counsel.

I wonder what type of words we've released to find ourselves in our present reality. William Booth, the founder of the Salvation Army, was interviewed and asked what were his concerns for the church of the next century. Here's what he said:

> In answer to your inquiry, I consider that the chief dangers which
> confront the coming century will be religion without the Holy
> Ghost, Christianity without Christ, forgiveness without repent-
> ance, salvation without regeneration, politics without God, and
> heaven without hell.[8]

When I read this prophetic warning, my heart was pierced as surely as if it had been thrust through with the point of a sword. I do not ache for the errors of others but for errors of my own. Now is not the time to divide camps and point fingers. The condition of the body of Christ is too desperate.

If what we have declared over the last few decades created this current reality, let's be intentional about constructing a new framework built on the solid rock of God's Word.

> The words of the reckless pierce like swords,
>   but the tongue of the wise brings healing. (Proverbs 12:18, NIV)

Let's speak God's wisdom and watch the healing begin.

Warnings

So many things in life come with a warning label, and words definitely come with multiple cautions. *Warning:* death and life are in the power of your words. *Warning:* be slow to speak. *Warning:* thoughts and words create your reality.

> *Watch your thoughts; they become words. Watch your*
> *words; they become actions. Watch your actions; they*
> *become habits. Watch your habits; they become character.*
> *Watch your character; it becomes your destiny.*
> —UNKNOWN

As powerful as this quote is, it could position us to live in a state of constantly policing our thoughts, words, actions, and habits! This progression is true, but we don't need to live in a police state where our thoughts are constantly edited. Instead, God invites us to exchange our thoughts and ways for his, which, by the way, is so much easier than figuring it out on our own!

> For my thoughts are not your thoughts,
>   neither are your ways my ways, declares the LORD.

For as the heavens are higher than the earth,

    so are my ways higher than your ways

    and my thoughts than your thoughts.

For as the rain and the snow come down from heaven

    and do not return there but water the earth,

making it bring forth and sprout,

    giving seed to the sower and bread to the eater,

so shall my word be that goes out from my mouth;

    it shall not return to me empty,

but it shall accomplish that which I purpose,

    and shall succeed in the thing for which I sent it.

      (Isaiah 55:8–11)

As we read his Word, it renews our minds. As our minds are renewed, our thoughts change. This change in our thought patterns produces a change in what we say about ourselves, our world, and others. This change in our language produces a change in our actions and connects us with heaven's purposes for the earth. Our words begin to echo the will of our Father in heaven, and the vineyard begins to flourish.

God's living Word is the origin of all the powerful, transformative truths. Ultimately, the Truth is not a theory to be debated; he is the Word made flesh—Jesus.

Jesus said to him, "I am the way, and the truth, and the life. No one comes to the Father except through me." (John 14:6)

There's a vast difference between telling the truth and being the truth! We are to follow his example of living the truth. He is the truth without an expiration date, because he is alive forevermore! One encourages you in the moment; the other transforms you with its light and momentum.

My phrase—"Your past is not your future!"—could be likened to a door partially opened; his Word is a gate thrown wide open. God's truth has the power to set you apart and clothe you in light. How awesome that our Father not only gave us a language but gave us Jesus, the example of how to live what we speak.

> Jesus said to them, "Truly, truly, I say to you, the Son can do
> nothing of his own accord, but only what he sees the Father
> doing. For whatever the Father does, that the Son does likewise."
> (John 5:19)

Not only is his Word alive…it is his will. How can I say this? Because Jesus showed the will of the Father, and he is God's Word expressed in human flesh.

Consequently, when Christ came into the world, he said,

> Sacrifices and offerings you have not desired,
> >   but a body have you prepared for me;
> in burnt offerings and sin offerings
> >   you have taken no pleasure.
> Then I said, *"Behold, I have come to do your will, O God,*
> >   *as it is written of me in the scroll of the book."* (Hebrews
> >   10:5–7, emphasis added)

So the question arises—what is written of us in the scroll of the book? According to Acts 2, God's daughters will be part of these heaven-breathed exploits: we will prophesy alongside his sons as we experience an outpouring of God's Spirit. We will serve him under the canopy of a sky set with wonders as we walk upon an earth filled with his signs. In our day all who call out to God will be saved (see verses 17–21). This marvelous framework outlines his generous will for us.

Do you want to do his will so all that was written of you will be something to behold? I believe you do. Let's seize this moment and seal it in prayer.

● ● ●

Heavenly Father,

Behold your daughter. I have come to do your will.
May all that was written of me be realized in my life
as I lay hold of your Word by speaking and expressing
it through my life. In Jesus's name, amen.

9

Sword of Harvest

Look, I tell you, lift up your eyes, and see
that the fields are white for harvest.

—John 4:35

There is only one sword native to North American soil, and in true American style, it is all-purpose, with more than twenty uses. The diverse applications of the machete can be divided into four main categories: clear and maintain paths, change environments, manage harvests, and kill or defend.

Here's a sampling of ways the machete can be used. It slices paths and maintains trails, chops compost to nurture a garden, or cuts tinder and wood for a fire. A machete can clear an area for a campsite, create a copse or grove, and diversify habitats by mowing lawns and carving out hedges. It's been known to prune trees and wayward vines to direct and encourage future growth; fashion poles, teepees, and trellis systems; and construct shelters. The machete is used to reap rice, sugarcane, corn, rye, millet, barley, buckwheat, oats, and livestock fodder, as well as cut down and split open coconuts, nuts, and more. The machete is ideal for removing above-ground vegetation while leaving the root biomass in place for future harvests.

Lastly, there is the protection and slaughter dynamic. Though it is not the original purpose of its design, the machete is a formidable weapon for self-defense, capable of fending off assailants and wild animals and killing venomous snakes. It also can be used to slaughter game or livestock.

Who knew…right?

The machete is comparable to combining a knife, an ax, and a sword, and because it has so many uses, this sword is part of everyday life in many parts of the world. Seriously, with such an impressive list of uses, I wonder how I've survived this long without one!

In the pages that follow, I am going to focus on what can happen as we clear paths, change environments, and harvest fields. You can find your way, create a refuge, and enjoy the fruit of your labor. And, along the way, you may encounter some snakes that need a quick dispatch.

Clearing and Maintaining Paths

Nothing illuminates a spiritual path more dramatically than the Word of God. Stroll through the book of Proverbs, and you will discover clarity for what lies before and behind you. Paths are not merely a means to an end. Paths and journeys have purpose. Sometimes arriving too quickly is detrimental. It is dangerous to arrive without our character mature or intact. Character and strength often come through staying the course. Proverbs 20:21 warns us that what is gotten quickly is not always blessed in the end.

With all our streamlined modes of transportation, we have lost some of our connection to the purpose of a path. A rich life and relationships are not built by jumping from point A to point B as quickly as possible but by gleaning the lessons of the journey.

In our day of sidewalks, paths are little more than dirt trails or short-cuts through forests and fields. In days gone by, though, it was under-stood that roads transported people but pathways connected them. Sadly, we have become a people who move from one place to another so quickly that we fail to blaze the trails we need to connect with others. And this constant horizontal movement across the face of the earth often comes at the expense of our vertical path.

It was no accident that one strategy Rome used to conquer the world was the construction of bridges and roads. These enabled the Romans to move their armies and export their culture. By design, roadways, bridges, and paths are neutral, but as in the days of Rome, hostile forces can use these roads as easily as the friendly allies. In our day digital paths encircle the globe. The Internet and social media serve as virtual roads and path-ways. But paths of social media should be forged with great care and not be used as a substitute for personal contact. Many marriages have been compromised because one spouse was alone in bed while the other was emotionally engaged with virtual intimates on the Internet. Who hasn't been with friends (or been the friend) who disengaged from conversation because the phone couldn't be set aside?

Each day is a journey on the course of time. We move through time even if we never leave our houses. Like time, careers and destinies have paths, friendships run their courses, and families have journeys. In addi-tion to the challenge of blazing trails, there is the need to keep what was forged unobstructed. This assures that others will not lose their way or become entangled due to our neglect.

Let us simplify matters. According to Psalms and Proverbs, there are ultimately only two paths in this course of life: one that ascends to light and life and another that descends to darkness and death. There is no middle way. The choice seems obvious…choose God's way to light and life. But there are seasons in life when we need some extra light in order to choose the right path.

For example, in seasons of youth, we naturally lack experience. In seasons of pain, we may lose perspective. In seasons of darkness, we may lose our way. Sometimes the entrance is poorly marked or the course dimly lit, and the need for additional light becomes glaringly apparent. Borrowing from the wisdom of the psalmist, we learn, "The entrance of thy words giveth light; it giveth understanding unto the simple" (Psalm 119:130, kjv).

This means we are not limited by the light level of our environment. As God's Word enters our hearts, it not only guides our souls, but it also provides light. What is dangerous in the dark is exposed in the light.

New and Ancient Paths

More than ever God is asking us to forge new trails and reopen the ancient paths. For far too long God's people have wandered off the highway to holiness (see Jeremiah 18:15). We need his Word in order to work out the way before us. Just as a machete clears paths in the wild, the sword of God's Word has the power to sever what entangles us.

More than ever God is asking us to forge new trails and reopen the ancient paths.

This means we may be led down paths that initially look more difficult, but we can use the Word of God to clear and light our steps as we go. If you are a Christian, the enemy was not able to block your entrance into the way of salvation, but he will work hard to get you off course. The light of God's Word grants discretion, which is capable of…

> delivering you from *the way of evil,*
>> from men of *perverted speech,*
> who forsake the *paths of uprightness*
>> to walk in the *ways of darkness,*
> who rejoice in doing evil
>> and delight in the perverseness of evil,
> men whose *paths are crooked,*
>> and who are *devious in their ways.* (Proverbs 2:12–15,
>>> emphasis added)

From these verses we learn that perversity of speech eventually leads to perverse ways and crooked paths, and these courses ultimately separate you from the way of life. This scripture shows three things: *evil has a way, a path, and a language.* So it stands to reason that righteousness has a way, a path, and a language (which, of course, you already knew!).

The term *way* speaks of a set of methods, customs, manners, techniques, tactics, and style or fashion. A sampling of evil's methods or ways would include pride, disobedience, dishonor, slander, perversity, lying, fornication, adultery, idolatry, vengefulness, hate, envy, wrath, and witchcraft.

The term *path* differs from *way* because *way* is the manner in which you travel, and *path* is the course to where you are headed. The *way* you get somewhere could range from walking to flying, while your *path* of travel might be from west to east. In context of the Scriptures, the way of traveling righteous paths is by telling the truth rather than lying.

And the third dynamic in this scripture is *language.* Whether we realize it or not, what we say will determine both our method of travel and our destination. Language has the power to connect and transport us to righteous paths and ways just as surely as our words have the power to separate us from evil.

In summary, *the way* describes *how* you journey, *the path* is your *route*, and both of these are often chosen by virtue of the words we speak. Our language or choice of words has the power to set the course of our lives.

But what if you are trying to find your path? What if an old one is overgrown or you want to maintain one so that others will find their way? How do you navigate these trails? Granted, many have lost their way because they were misled. Legalism discourages far too many from true godliness, while the course of lawlessness likewise ensnares those who journey it with lust and raging passions. It makes no sense to tread the very paths that led others to nowhere. We have a chance to walk in a new and living way (see Hebrews 10:20).

> *Do not go where the path may lead, go instead*
> *where there is no path and leave a trail.*
> —RALPH WALDO EMERSON

I don't mean this to sound contradictory, but sometimes righteous paths require an unconventional approach. Jesus never diverted from the path of righteousness, but he was definitely a trailblazer. He commissioned those who followed him to do the same when he sent his disciples into *all* the earth to make disciples in every nation. Before the Cross, all paths to salvation led to the temple in Jerusalem. After his glorious resurrection, Calvary became the epicenter for temples of flesh and blood scattered throughout the earth. Both Martin Luther and Mother Teresa abandoned an expected route in order to leave a trail for others.

The way you leave the path is also the way to return to one—you wait on God's directive, then follow where he leads in both word and deed. We read his Word, ponder his ways, and speak his language, and what we seek will open up before us. Through the power of his Word, he makes a way where there seemed to be no way. Our God knows how to navigate the roadless expanse of a sandy wilderness or a body of water.

Barricade the road that goes Nowhere;
  grace me with your clear revelation.
I choose the true road to Somewhere,
  I post your road signs at every curve and corner.
I grasp and cling to whatever you tell me;
  GOD, don't let me down!
I'll run the course you lay out for me
  if you'll just show me how. (Psalm 119:29–32, MSG)

Change Environments

Another function of the machete is its ability to shape or fashion a new environment.

Many years ago John and I built a home in the midst of heavily treed Florida lots. As they bulldozed and cleared our lot, all the rodents, pests, snakes, and scorpions from our area headed for the two flanking fields. We opened up a spot for the house and lawn by changing the immediate environment, but this did not mean the former inhabitants of our area went away…just that they were displaced.

When the devil had ended every temptation, he departed from
him until an opportune time.
  And Jesus returned in the power of the Spirit to Galilee, and
a report about him went out through all the surrounding country.
(Luke 4:13–14)

Not only had Jesus fasted in the wilderness, but he had faced off with Satan. He was spent but not empty. He returned filled with the power of the Holy Spirit. Fasting is more than not eating. It is a time when we determine what will have preeminence and voice in our lives. We empty ourselves so that he might fill us.

Sometimes you need to make a radical environmental change—turn off your television, get off the Internet, and hang up the phone. When all these voices are silenced, you have a chance to quiet yourself as well. However, this isn't an invitation to meditate on a deeper revelation of you but to experience a deeper revelation of him.

> He who dwells in the shelter of the Most High
> > will abide in the shadow of the Almighty.
> I will say to the LORD, "My refuge and my fortress,
> > my God, in whom I trust." (Psalm 91:1–2)

You can see your life in a similar manner. When Jesus came in and cleared the decks of your life, the enemy did not disappear; he just moved aside. He was not gone; he was simply out of sight, watching for an opportunity to reestablish himself. To avoid a hostile reinvasion, you must firmly establish a new lifestyle and environment. Listen to the way God instructed Israel to proceed as it entered the environment of the Promised Land.

> You shall do what is right and good in the sight of the LORD, that
> it may go well with you, and that you may go in and take posses-
> sion of the good land that the LORD swore to give to your fathers
> by thrusting out all your enemies from before you, as the LORD
> has promised. (Deuteronomy 6:18–19)

Our Lord thrusts out the opposition and gives us the task of possessing or occupying the land. Evil is overcome or displaced by good as surely as darkness is displaced by light. Jesus is the Savior of the world, and it is up to us to take this gospel and invade and occupy our earth with his love.

> Behold, I have given you authority to tread on serpents and scorpions, and over all the power of the enemy, and nothing shall hurt you. Nevertheless, do not rejoice in this, that the spirits are subject to you, but rejoice that your names are written in heaven. (Luke 10:19–20)

Okay, far too often this scripture has been used to justify snake handling to prove one's spiritual authority. This practice is prideful, stupid, and often fatal. We are not supposed to wrap ourselves in snakes any more than we'd wrap ourselves in the power of the enemy. We have authority to tread, not hold! We are to crush rather than cuddle.

Manage Harvests

In times of harvest, paths must be cleared and maintained so the harvesters can get to the fields.

> Do you not say, "There are yet four months, then comes the harvest"? Look, I tell you, lift up your eyes, and see that the fields are white for harvest. Already the one who reaps is receiving wages and gathering fruit for eternal life, so that sower and reaper may rejoice together. For here the saying holds true, "One sows and another reaps." I sent you to reap that for which you did not

labor. Others have labored, and you have entered into their labor.
(John 4:35–38)

Harvest is a short season of urgency, and all that we hold in our
hands must be wielded for more than one purpose. Our days could be
likened to the days of Nehemiah when he defended as he built. Likewise
we defend as we harvest.

> Proclaim this among the nations:
> Consecrate for war;
>   stir up the mighty men.
> Let all the men of war draw near;
>   let them come up.
> Beat your plowshares into swords,
>   and your pruning hooks into spears;
>   let the weak say, "I am a warrior." (Joel 3:9–10)

Often those who do not participate in the harvest will try to make
rivals out of those who do. Rivalries have been a problem since Cain and
Abel battled for God's approval. Competition has its place in the Olym-
pics but not in the house of God. Jesus and John were co-laborers who
refused to be pitted against each other. They understood that what they
were doing was more important than their popularity.

When Jesus made his appearance on the banks of the Jordan, John
the Baptist had been crying out and directing the nation of Judea toward
a path of repentance through baptism and the confession of sin. When
Jesus came out to likewise be baptized by him, John protested (see Matthew 3:13–15). John understood he was but the herald and Jesus was the
heralded. When the two of them submitted to this process, the heavens

opened up, God's voice was heard, and Jesus was declared God's Son (see verses 16–17).

After Jesus spent forty days in the wilderness, he and his disciples began to baptize alongside John and his disciples. The Pharisees and Sadducees came out to watch and keep score.

> Jesus realized that the Pharisees were keeping count of the baptisms that he and John performed (although his disciples, not Jesus, did the actual baptizing). They had posted the score that Jesus was ahead, turning him and John into rivals in the eyes of the people. So Jesus left the Judean countryside and went back to Galilee. (John 4:1–3, MSG)

In seasons of harvest it is better to leave a field than to allow those who are not under the authority of the Lord of the harvest to make you rivals.

Jesus decided to journey back to Galilee and discovered a ripe field on the way! Exhausted and thirsty, Jesus stopped at a well where a promiscuous woman found him when she went to draw water. Later her testimony opened up the Samaritan town of Sychar (see verses 4–30).

When the religious leaders couldn't get John and Jesus to be rivals with each other, they positioned them as rivals among the people. Rivalry and competition always attempt to put people in the position where they have to side with one group or the other.

John was a forerunner who understood his season and purpose.

Fencing Fact

In sword fighting, maintaining formation is essential. Otherwise, allies are in danger from each other, because they are fighting in close quarters.

Forerunners do not split the field. Like him, we should herald the One
to come.

Kill or Defend

When environments are changed and paths are cut into former wil-
dernesses, often snakes appear. If we see evil revealed, we do not engage it
in our human strength. We slay it with the machete of God's Word...*it
is written!* The very acts of taking land and freeing the inhabitants tread
upon serpents and scorpions.

In addition to the wilderness and any environment overgrown with
foliage, fields are common hiding places for venomous snakes. The tall
stalks of barley mask their holes and hide their movements.

You could say that harvesttime is the combination of changing environments and creating paths. Harvesters work to release the grain in the
row that stands before them, while the gatherers collect the produce that
follows their labor. If a predator appears in the field and threatens either
the harvester or the harvest, it must be struck down. This job falls to the
reaper, not the gatherer, because you cannot fight with full arms. This
means that the implement of harvesting quickly becomes a tool of self-
defense. Even if the snake is not positioned to strike, it must be removed.

Never allow a danger your labors have exposed to slip unchecked or
unheralded into the field of another. If you see it, address it. If you are
not equipped to address it, then warn others there is a snake in the fields.

●　●　●

So let's bring the Word of God like a machete back into this picture and
clear the way before us, change our environment to one that is conducive
to harvest, and deal with any snakes that would cut across our paths.

• • •

Dear Heavenly Father,

Direct my paths by the light of your Word, and instruct me in ways to leave a clearly marked trail behind for others. I want to use your Word to create environments that encourage others to flourish. I choose to guard my heart so as not to mistake co-laborers for competitors.

Open my eyes to see the fields surrounding my life that are white and ready for harvest. In Jesus's name, amen.

10

Sword of Light

For now we see in a mirror dimly, but then
face to face. Now I know in part; then I shall
know fully, even as I have been fully known.

—1 Corinthians 13:12

In the real world, a sword of light doesn't yet exist except in the form of lasers. However, in the *Star Wars* universe, there is some futuristic imagery I would like to borrow—the light saber. This weapon liberates what it illuminates.

Jesus is our light at the end of a very long and dark tunnel, and when we see him, we will be like him.

Our vantage from this earthbound temporal realm is at best dimly lit, limited, and distant, but when eternity swallows time, we will see fully, face to face, in a realm without shadow. This means that now we can't see the whole picture. Yet there has never been a more desperate need for us to perceive or discern what we do see accurately.

As the saying goes, there is *more than what meets the eye*, thus we need the sword of light and discernment. I discover more when my eyes are open wide than when I squint. Often the things I see when I am not predisposed to the obvious are the truest.

We live in a season pregnant with expectancy and warnings.

We live in a time when light is distinctly highlighted by gross shadow. Throughout the New Testament the believers are warned that the earth's last days will yield an environment rife with offense, false teaching, and everything else that breeds deception. Paul described our day to Timothy this way:

> You should know this, Timothy, that in the last days there will be very difficult times. For people will love only themselves and their money. They will be boastful and proud, scoffing at God, disobedient to their parents, and ungrateful. They will consider nothing sacred. They will be unloving and unforgiving; they will slander others and have no self-control. They will be cruel and hate what is good. They will betray their friends, be reckless, be puffed up with pride, and love pleasure rather than God. They will act religious, but they will reject the power that could make them godly. Stay away from people like that! (2 Timothy 3:1–5, NLT)

If Timothy needed to know about our condition two thousand years ago, how much more do we now need a heightened awareness of our time? Notice Paul doesn't say our difficulties will be due to economic collapse, earthquakes, and wars. The condition of the earth, her nations, or their banks is not what strains our time. Our struggle arises from a darkened condition of the human heart.

Woven throughout the New Testament are warnings to *beware, take heed, watch out, be on guard, be alert,* and *give careful attention to God's Word and our doctrine.* Not only are we warned against false teachers; we're warned about the dangers of self-deception.

But living in constant fear of deception will likewise lead you down the wrong road. Living in fear leads to awful decisions, because fear gives horrible counsel (unless it is the fear of the Lord). God never gave you a spirit of fear. He gave you a "spirit...of power, and of love, and of a sound mind" (2 Timothy 1:7, KJV). This spirit gift has exactly the three qualities you will need to walk in discernment and wield the Word of God appropriately.

The Word of God is the lamp that lights our paths while it judges our actions as surely as it discerns our hearts. Without the light of God's Word, we would all be running around in the dark, afraid of what we cannot see.

> The unfolding of your words gives light;
>   it imparts understanding to the simple. (Psalm 119:130)

I love the imagery captured here. As we unfold or spread out the Word of God like a treasure map, we gain perspective and insight. Other Bible versions incorporate the terms "break open," "the teaching of," and "the entrance of."

Without the insight of God's Word, it is easy to mistake an enemy for a friend and someone's past for their future, because the shadow realm distorts our perspective. But when light is brought to a situation, you see what is actually before you.

> For the word of God is living and active, sharper than any two-
> edged sword, piercing to the division of soul and of spirit, of joints
> and of marrow, and discerning the thoughts and intentions of the
> heart. (Hebrews 4:12)

Therefore, our tempering must go far deeper than what is seen. This means that our involuntary core must be strengthened. What use are muscled arms that hold a sword to the throat of an ally or strong legs that hold the wrong ground? We are nothing if our hearts and souls fail us, if our strength alone succeeds.

As I studied the art of fencing, I learned good fencers see what is coming. They instinctively know the move their opponent will make next, and they adjust their posture to counter the attack. In the following verse Paul was writing the church in Corinth and charging them to reaffirm their love for a brother who had been formerly disciplined—"so that we would not be outwitted by Satan; for we are not ignorant of his designs" (2 Corinthians 2:11).

Overcoming Satan's Designs

What are the enemy's schemes designed to do? To divide us from God and each other through the isolation tactics of guilt, judgment, shame, and suspicion. We counter this attack with love, power, and a sound mind.

First, *love:*

> It is my prayer that your love may abound more and more, with knowledge and all discernment. (Philippians 1:9)

Where love is stunted, the darkness of deception abounds; where love flourishes, knowledge and discernment increase proportionally. I can honestly say I have never had someone speak knowledge and discernment into my life who did not first love me.

> Whoever says [she] is in the light and hates [her] brother [or sister] is still in darkness. Whoever loves [her] brother [or sister]

abides in the light, and in [her] there is no cause for stumbling. But whoever hates [her] brother [or sister] is in the darkness and walks in the darkness, and does not know where [she] is going, because the darkness has blinded [her] eyes. (1 John 2:9–11)

It is pretty simple: hate lives in the dark; love lives in the light. Haters stumble as they walk in the dark, clueless about where they are headed because they are blinded (self-deceived). Lovers walk in the light, know where they are headed, and get there without stumbling.

In these areas of finesse and intuition, women have an advantage. One way God's daughters can tone their intuitive core and maintain the balance of discernment is…the practice of love. So here's some core discernment training (from 1 Corinthians 13:4–7):

1. Love doesn't react; it is patient and kind.
2. Love doesn't keep a list of past sins.
3. Love trusts God, so it endures.
4. Love celebrates truth.
5. Love doesn't consult the past.
6. Love looks for the best.
7. Love extends itself into the future.

The second step is *authority* or *power.*

There is no authority without power, and no legitimate power without authority. Ultimately, both of these are gifts from God. To realize both, you must know your position.

But you are a chosen race, a royal priesthood, a holy nation, a people for his own possession, that you may proclaim the excellencies of him who called you out of darkness into his marvelous light. (1 Peter 2:9)

Regardless of your natural lineage or job description, this is your true assignment. In Christ, you are a chosen race of daughters, descendants of a royal priesthood, and ambassadors of a holy nation. You are his prized possession, redeemed to proclaim all that he did when he called you out of a life of darkness to live forever in the glory of his light. That's the power of your testimony.

It is pretty simple: hate lives in the dark; love lives in the light.

Then there is the third element of *a clear and sound mind.*

What does it mean to have a sound mind? *Merriam-Webster* defines *sound* as being free of injury, disease, flaw, error, or defect; the ability to reason logically; reasonable and both well founded and well grounded. Only God could give his people this perspective in the midst of a world that is so broken, unhealthy, and diseased in all its reasoning processes. The Word of God has the power to renew your mind and change it from unsound to sound. Encounters with the Word can change you as surely as the one encounter with Jesus changed a naked, violent madman into someone who was clothed, calm, and sound of mind (see Mark 5:1–15).

It is impossible to be discerning when your mind is tempest tossed. Discernment means our diet moves from the milk of God's Word to a more solid diet that gives strength to those who know how to digest it. This comes through renewing our minds by the light of his Word, as well as by exercising discernment.

> But solid food is for the mature, for those who have their powers
> of discernment trained by constant practice to distinguish good
> from evil. (Hebrews 5:14)

There was a time that I viewed this scripture's meaning with suspicion. Before you fall into the mire of the misunderstanding that tripped me up, know that this verse does not equate discernment with judging. There is a much bigger idea in play here than assessing others as guilty or not guilty. Maturity, discernment, and strength can be found in the Word, and we will need all of these working together if we are going to navigate these waters safely and distinguish good from evil.

More Than Meets the Eye

Discernment comes with maturity, which is ultimately about our approach to life. In truth, we can be mature or immature at any age or stage of life. We do not grow in discernment by labeling people and things. Just as my keyboarding speed always slows when I look to see the letters on the keys, labels keep us from moving freely in faith and trusting that something unseen will carry us. After a while, keyboarding is about feeling the keys rather than seeing them.

The truth is, there is always far more than the obvious. We know that all we now see was made by what we cannot yet see.

> *Every natural fact is a symbol*
> *of some spiritual fact.*
> —Ralph Waldo Emerson

Likewise, discernment in this life is not an exercise in labeling one type of person, thing, or experience as "good" and other people, things, or events as "bad."

Discernment is about knowing what really is going on so that heroic daughters can turn what others see as a disadvantage into an advantage. The discerning warrior will know how to turn evil around for good.

Discernment could be likened to distinguishing a light in the distance. In our present culture at times the lines between good and evil seem blurred. We have so much darkness right in front of us that it obscures the light on the horizon.

To accurately see, we must look within and listen to the inner voice of our hearts. It is from there that we draw upon the Holy Spirit's counsel. Notice that discernment is a power that must be trained through constant practice. Only then will we be able to separate or distinguish good from evil.

> *Treat people as if they were what they ought to be, and*
> *help them to become what they are capable of being.*
> —JOHANN WOLFGANG VON GOETHE

Let me open the pages of my life as an example. In the past I lived an immoral, sexually promiscuous life. Those who were skilled in the art of labeling took one look at me and stamped "sexual train wreck" on my forehead. But describing the wrapping of a package doesn't mean you know the contents. For many years my life was marked and masked by what I had done. But thankfully God placed a father figure in my life who had mastered the art of discernment.

Fencing Fact

Timing is the single most important component in fencing.

He and his wife welcomed me into their home. When I spent the night at their house, I felt welcome and safe, while in other homes I just felt watched. He and his wife looked beyond an obviously broken girl and saw into the realm of what might be.

They understood that even though I had derailed my sexual life, if it could be put back on track, my past might light the way for others. Rather than act as though my past had never happened, they encouraged me to light the tinder of it as a beacon for others. Where others saw only a failure, they saw someone with so many potential bonfires that could be used to redeem others!

Over time I was able to extract the good from my evil. I redeemed my choices by way of example so others would not journey down the same road.

We need to mature in our ability to discern. True discernment understands that the shadowed darkness of one's past can serve as a distant light in someone else's future. Warriors look beyond the dark past and obvious present to see a glorious revelation in the future for themselves and others! Jesus came as "a light for revelation to the Gentiles, and for glory to your people Israel" (Luke 2:32).

However, please do not imagine I am naive and unaware of the need to discern when darkness is masked in light. This ability to distinguish good fruit from bad fruit is an increasingly necessary skill:

> Each tree is known by its own fruit. For figs are not gathered from
> thornbushes, nor are grapes picked from a bramble bush. The
> good person out of the good treasure of his heart produces good,
> and the evil person out of his evil treasure produces evil, for out of
> the abundance of the heart his mouth speaks. (Luke 6:44–45)

Apparently the most accurate indicator of what is stored within us is what comes out of our mouths! Sometimes a person can say something that sounds right, but it feels wrong. Other times a person will say something that sounds wrong, but it will feel right (such as with young, raw Christians). Listen with your heart—then listen to your heart. Don't violate your inner sense.

So, giving a nod to the obvious, this type of response is not developed through physical training; it runs much deeper. It is an intuitive, perceptive response. And this is an area where women can shine. When hearts have been tempered and the poison of suspicion has been purged, we are in a position to notice what we might otherwise miss.

Discernment and Prayer

What does intercession look like? Is it simply a matter of praying?

Well, I believe intercession should always begin with prayer, but true intercession rarely ends there. Some words that frame the definition of *intercede* are "intervene, mediate, negotiate, arbitrate"—and my favorite—"arise." So some of the ways we intercede are to speak up for another as an advocate, speak into a conflict that needs resolution, and stand up for the downtrodden and silenced. The Word shows us when we should get involved, where to find our answers, and ways to right what's been wronged, and it directs us to the light at the end of the path.

> *God never gives us discernment in order that*
> *we may criticize, but that we may intercede.*
> —OSWALD CHAMBERS

Given this understanding of *intercession,* we realize more fully what it means to intercede. I believe intercession happens whenever light encounters darkness.

Jesus came as the mediator between God and humanity, and he intervened whenever he encountered the dark forces of sickness, demonic possession, religious distortion, and oppression. He negotiated the religious double-talk of the law experts as he brilliantly arbitrated with astounding wisdom. And even before he rose from the grave, he rose to every occasion to lift others.

When Jesus was confronted with a woman accused of adultery, he rose up in intercession, because he discerned the religious leaders had brought her to trick and trap him. They were twisting God's Word into an instrument of judgment. In this intercessory challenge he discerned the real issue and spoke light into their darkened hearts:

> As they continued to ask him, he stood up and said to them, "Let him who is without sin among you be the first to throw a stone at her." (John 8:7)

Then Jesus bent back down, waited until all the accusers were gone, and rose to his feet again:

> Jesus stood up and said to her, "Woman, where are they? Has no one condemned you?" She said, "No one, Lord." And Jesus said, "Neither do I condemn you; go, and from now on sin no more."
>
> Again Jesus spoke to them, saying, "I am the light of the world. Whoever follows me will not walk in darkness, but will have the light of life." (verses 10–12)

He empowered her to walk sinless in the light of her future—the very thing she could never do while still trapped and tethered to the dark condemnation of her past. Stones would no longer send this nameless woman to the grave!

Sisters, let's lay down our stones of judgment and pick up a sword of light. Discernment has the power to light the world for others.

Jesus also interceded when he stood before the entrance of a stone grave and raised Lazarus from the dead. Jesus wept out of the anguish of love for a friend. Then he prayed:

> Jesus lifted up his eyes and said, "Father, I thank you that you have heard me. I knew that you always hear me, but I said this

on account of the people standing around, that they may believe that you sent me." When he had said these things, he cried out with a loud voice, "Lazarus, come out." The man who had died came out, his hands and feet bound with linen strips, and his face wrapped with a cloth. Jesus said to them, "Unbind him, and let him go." (John 11:41–44)

Lazarus left behind the darkness of the tomb and found release in the light of a new day. Discernment and true intercession have the power to release restrained captives into their destiny.

Throughout his earthly walk, Jesus discerned the work of the Evil One, then interceded by bringing light, truth, and healing into the darkened days of earth. In my opinion the most dramatic work of discernment was when Jesus said, "Father, forgive them, for they know not what they do" (Luke 23:34).

Discernment realizes when others are blind and then intercedes based on their ignorance rather than on their actions. The Cross ended our separation from God, but his intercession didn't stop there. Jesus not only rose from the grave; he ascended into heaven:

Who shall bring any charge against God's elect? It is God who justifies. Who is to condemn? Christ Jesus is the one who died— more than that, who was raised—who is at the right hand of God, who indeed is interceding for us. (Romans 8:33–34)

And because of his perpetual, risen, and discerning posture, we are promised,

Who shall separate us from the love of Christ? Shall tribulation, or distress, or persecution, or famine, or nakedness, or danger, or sword?… No, in all these things we are more than conquerors through him who loved us. (verses 35, 37)

Lovely Ones, it is time to strengthen ourselves in the Word and light this world with true discernment and arise in the light of the actions of intercession.

• • •

Heavenly Father,

I am ready to lay down the stones of judgment and become a discerning daughter. I will renew my mind by reading, speaking, and living your Word in light. I want to see heaven's light and counsel invade the darkness of earth. I am ready to set free those who are captives to sin, by declaring light and love into their future. I am willing to weep over those who have been buried in graves of human trafficking, religious bondage, and despair. I will lift my voice, extend my hands, stand up, and step in on behalf of others. In Jesus's name, amen.

11

Sword of Song

Sing and rejoice, O daughter of Zion,
for behold, I come and I will dwell
in your midst, declares the LORD.

—Zechariah 2:10

A sword is balanced like a tuning instrument... Sometimes all it takes is a song to tip the battle in your favor.

You don't have to be a worship leader to worship, and you do not have to be a singer to sing. You only need to be a daughter, which is a good thing, because there are many battles you win in song.

I was very excited when I found a sword with a shape and function that captures the imagery of what happens as we sing. It is an ancient sword called the flamberge, which literally means "flame blade."[9] The edges of this sword have an undulating, or waved, pattern. When the blade makes contact with another sword's blade, the flamberge's design transfers vibrations to the opponent's sword, making it shake and tremble in the other's hand. This weakens the opponent's grip, and an increase in friction creates an advantage for the bearer of the flamberge.

How crazy is all that?

I truly believe that, as we sing, the same things happen...especially as we sing the Word! The airwaves begin to vibrate with sound, and the

grip of the enemy slips as the friction between light and darkness increases. The enemy's onslaught is slowed, and curses and accusations are arrested or thrown into confusion. This heady combination of musical instruments and song has the power to alter, for good or for evil, the very environment that surrounds us.

In my own experience there have been moments of worship when it literally felt as though time itself slowed almost to a standstill.

And how ironic that it was a flaming blade rotating in every direction that blocked Adam's return to Eden (see Genesis 3:24). It would appear that through the dynamic of song and worship, a similar sword grants us entrance.

> Enter his gates with thanksgiving,
>   and his courts with praise!
> Give thanks to him; bless his name! (Psalm 100:4)

As we wield words of adoration and gratitude—often spoken as songs—heaven is accessed, and an audience in the courts of our Father is granted. We have spanned the vast expanse of the unseen realms and trodden the pavement of heaven—while our feet are still planted firmly on earth. I can't tell you how many times I have literally felt swept away as I walked the rooms of my home while singing.

We don't need a key or a letter of invitation to enter God's courts. All we need is a song!

Fencing Fact

"On guard" refers not only to a defensive attitude but also to an offensive one. It is, in effect, a position of readiness.

The Beginning of Song

Exodus 15 has the first mention of the dynamic of song. Before this, musical instruments are referred to, but not words.

> I will sing to the LORD, for he has triumphed gloriously;
>> the horse and his rider he has thrown into the sea.
> The LORD is my strength and my song,
>> and he has become my salvation;
> this is my God, and I will praise him,
>> my father's God, and I will exalt him.
> The LORD is a man of war;
>> the LORD is his name. (Exodus 15:1–3)

In this song of victory, Moses declared God was his song of strength.

Singing in ways that exalt God declares his reign over your life. Singing to him opens your heart and enlarges your life with his wonder. I can't even count the number of times when worshiping shifted my entire perspective. There are times when I feel overwhelmed by all that life throws my way. Maybe I just heard horrible news or an awful report that threatens to frighten me. If the attack is intense enough, I will go behind closed doors and not only sing but dance as well until I sense a song covering my situation.

Then there are other times when I feel underwhelmed, even lethargic. Sometimes life on the road is a bit disorienting, but there is one constant. When I get to my room after traveling all day by planes and cars, I arrest the atmosphere with worship. As soon as possible, I pray over my room and put my headphones on.

By way of praise and worship songs, I can experience the atmosphere of heaven no matter where I am on earth. I know at such times that I have come to minister, and I refuse to allow a dreary hotel room in a city far from home to discourage me. Or maybe the room is lovely but I feel spent and empty of strength and spirit, and rather than head off to speak at a service, I'd like to just take a nap. Then I know it is time to stir up the gift.

> Be filled with the Spirit, addressing one another in psalms and hymns and spiritual songs, singing and making melody to the Lord with your heart, giving thanks always and for everything to God the Father in the name of our Lord Jesus Christ. (Ephesians 5:18–20)

As we sing, God is magnified. His dominion is declared over our situation. As he inhabits the praises of his people, we are before him even as he is within us. Our hearts begin to swell with his courage as they overflow with gratitude.

Songs of Battle

There was a time when the choir of Judah defeated three impossibly large armies that had assembled to destroy them (see 2 Chronicles 20). As God's holy people shouted and praised their invincible God, he threw the enemy armies into confusion and caused them to slaughter one another. And what was their strategic battle cry?

> Give thanks to the Lord,
>   for his love endures forever. (2 Chronicles 20:21, NIV)

What army can stand against the power of enduring love? Not one, because love cannot fail.

Another one of my favorite examples of God fighting on our behalf in the midst of a battle is told in Isaiah:

> And you will sing
>   as on the night you celebrate a holy festival;
> your hearts will rejoice
>   as when people playing pipes go up
> to the mountain of the LORD,
>   to the Rock of Israel.
> The LORD will *cause people to hear* his majestic voice
>   and *will make them see* his arm coming down
> with raging anger and consuming fire,
>   with cloudburst, thunderstorm and hail.
> The voice of the LORD will shatter Assyria;
>   with his rod he will strike them down.
> Every stroke the LORD lays on them
>   with his punishing club
> will be to the music of timbrels and harps,
>   as he fights them in battle with the blows of his arm.
>   (Isaiah 30:29–32, NIV, emphasis added)

My part in this equation is to *open my mouth and sing*! But not just any song will do. I am to sing as though it is a night on which I climb God's mountain, and from the lofty heights I recover his perspective and remember just how awesome the Most High is. As I sing with this type of joyful strength, God actually opens the ears and eyes of my spirit to hear his majestic voice and see his mighty arm raised in battle. His voice demolishes strongholds, even as his rod assails the enemy. All this happens in unison with the musical instruments of our day.

Why are we unsheathing our swords only halfway? When we worship in unified joy with all our strength and might, God routs the enemy with his sword.

As you know, we do not wrestle with enemies of flesh and blood. Our struggle is with the invisible forces of darkness that drive every action in this earth that is contrary to light, love, truth, faith, hope, and courage.

One of the most powerful collections of God's promises is in Isaiah 54. In this one chapter we find God's provision of legacy, increase, restoration, redemption, compassion, a sure foundation, freedom from fear, children discipled by God, and vindication from the enemy. And you can have it all for a song!

> "Sing, O barren one, who did not bear;
>   break forth into singing and cry aloud,
>   you who have not been in labor!
> For the children of the desolate one will be more
>   than the children of her who is married," says the LORD.
>   (Isaiah 54:1)

When you sing, the very portals of your life open up to heaven's provision. When I feel tethered, surrounded, limited, or even just earthbound, I pull out my sword of song and lift my voice.

And I dance as well. And why not? Dancing was the awkward activity that distinguished King David as God's man and at the same time brought about the desolation of his wife Michal:

> As the ark of the LORD came into the city of David, Michal the daughter of Saul looked out of the window and saw King David leaping and dancing before the LORD, and she despised him in her heart. (2 Samuel 6:16)

People are not your audience…God is. David couldn't help himself. His joy was uncontainable, so he danced wildly. The ark was back, and God's promise to him had been fulfilled. Music invites your body to move, but remembering all that God has done for you will move you. As you open the gates of your heart through intentional gratitude and words of thankful affirmation for everything he has done, you touch all that he is. Our songs in the night move him into our day. As you sing, the environment of your life will literally vibrate with a new frequency of expectancy, as the enemy's progress is arrested and you are ushered into God's presence.

When you sing, the very portals of your life open up to heaven's provision.

As we sing, he hears, and we begin to see the promises of God realized in our lives.

● ● ●

Dear Heavenly Father,

I am ready to sing over all the broken, barren places of my life. I believe that, as I sing, you will fill my heart with the expectancy of hope, and faith will arise as I express my love to you. You alone have the power to shatter the lies and strongholds of the enemy by the power of your royal reign and rule. Forgive me for withholding the glory that's due your name. From this moment forth I choose to be like that flaming sword that turns in every direction. And regardless of my circumstances, I will sing your praises and will sing of your love and mercy that endure forever. In Jesus's name, amen.

Sword of Silence

One sword keeps another in the sheath.

—George Herbert

The sword of silence is best captured in the imagery of a sword that remains within its scabbard. It is a sword contained and undrawn. The handle of this sword is visible, revealing that it could be grasped, but the blade is hidden, showing that the bearer has chosen to keep it encased.

Silence is a sword unseen because it is a word unspoken or an action untaken. When silence is required, the weapons you carry should remain concealed. This sword is relevant when we lay aside all we would or could do to save or defend ourselves. It is what happens when body and soul are laid at the very feet of our King.

Silence can mean many things. It can mean you truly have no answer to the question, accusation, or assault. Sometimes things come at us that we literally do not understand and, therefore, do not know how to respond to. Silence can also mean you have a response but have chosen not to give it voice. If the sword is not drawn, it would be because something has stilled our hands. I am not talking about being arrested by fear but about God whispering, "Leave this one to me." Remaining still often requires more strength than striking.

Stilled and silent is the best posture we can assume when we need to hear from God.

Then there are times when this stance becomes the best one we can adopt for God to be revealed to others. Both of these tactics require that we rule our souls. In our present culture this is referred to as self-control: "A man without self-control is like a city broken into and left without walls" (Proverbs 25:28).

If by our careless words or deeds we have left our souls unprotected, then a period of silent reflection and repentance can begin to right what was ransacked. (More on this later.)

There also are times when we find ourselves in the midst of threatening circumstances that are not of our making. We have obeyed God and followed his leading, only to find ourselves in an all-out struggle between light and darkness.

Perhaps our best biblical example of a "the odds are against you" and "this one is too big for you to handle" battle is when the children of Israel left behind Egypt, the land of their enslavement.

After a series of arduous back-and-forth exchanges of more than a few plagues and negotiations, God stepped in and released the destroyer, who killed the firstborn sons of Egypt. A grief-stricken Pharaoh freed the Israelites to go and worship their God. But God again hardened his heart, and Pharaoh changed his mind and sent the entire force of his army against the exiting Israelites.

Naturally, the Israelites were more than a little frightened as they beheld the chariots and horses bearing down on them. Rather than blame Pharaoh, they accused Moses of bringing them out to the desert to kill them! All seemed lost, and there appeared to be no way of escape. By all logical assessments they were trapped, with a vast sea looming before them and the world's finest army arrayed behind them. I bet you remember that our amazing God views ambushes without any means of escape as opportunities. Israel was right where God wanted them when Moses boldly declared:

> Fear not, stand firm, and see the salvation of the LORD, which he will work for you today. For the Egyptians whom you see today, you shall never see again. The LORD will fight for you, and you have only to be *silent.* (Exodus 14:13–14, emphasis added)

Do you agree that silence is challenging in moments of terror?

As I read these words, I remember the epic imagery of the movie *The Ten Commandments.* The swirling pillar of fire that had been leading them switched to the back of the group to block the Egyptian army. All night the wall of fire held the Egyptian army at bay. Meanwhile, the wind of God was busy parting the Red Sea and drying the sea floor, thus creating a mud-free path of escape.

As an observer I think, *This is shut-your-mouth awesome!*

But the wonder of this feat didn't stop there. After the Israelites had safely crossed over to the other side, the Egyptians felt compelled to follow. At the opportune moment God released the Red Sea waters and buried the entire Egyptian army in one fell swoop.

It is this feat without equal that inspired Moses to burst out in song and Miriam and all the women to join in with a tambourine dance!

Apparently, when the Lord fights for you, all you have to do is remain still and silent until it's time to celebrate. Sounds simple, right? Yes. But I am *not* going to say it is easy.

Many times I have nearly choked on what I didn't say. As you are already aware, most of the battles we face do not include an epic display of fire and water. There is no wind cutting a path through a visible sea. There is no pillar of fire to light our night and deny the enemy army access. Our enemy is not chasing us with chariots and spears. The attacks are more subtle, and more likely than not he is armed with lies of distortion, isolating rumors, and immobilizing fear.

The only salt water within a hundred miles may be the tears in our eyes, and the pillar of fire is a flickering flame in our hearts. And yet we are promised that he has our back, not because he's assigned angels, but because he is our rear guard. We have his assurance that he will never leave us or forsake us.

Let's look at Moses's admonishment again from some other angles.

Moses spoke to the people: "Don't be afraid. Stand firm and watch GOD do his work of salvation for you today. Take a good look at the Egyptians today for you're never going to see them again.

GOD will fight the battle for you.
And you? You keep your mouths shut!"
(Exodus 14:13–14, MSG)

And again,

Moses answered the people, "Do not be afraid. Stand firm and you will see the deliverance the LORD will bring you today. The Egyptians you see today you will never see again. The LORD will fight for you; you need only to be still." (verses 13–14, NIV)

There is a recurring pattern here. First and foremost, we are not to be afraid. We are to banish every aspect of fear from our minds and not allow it to muddy our thinking. Next, there is a charge to stand firm and hold our ground. This means we don't run, yield, or back down but instead remain upright just where we are. With these two elements in play, we are positioned to see God do the miraculous. He invites us to behold or, better yet, get ready to be amazed as we witness God's deliverance and salvation on our behalf.

I love how Moses changed a nation's perspective with imagery. "Take a last look at this enemy because you will not see them again. And while this awesome display of God's might and faithfulness unfolds, you are charged to be still and silent. There is to be no mocking, no screaming, no questions—just silence as you drink it all in."

When battles or adversaries are too big for us to handle, God has an opportunity to make himself known as deliverer. We back off, and he steps in and reveals his might, faithfulness, and power.

From this account in Exodus, we learn that God deliberately and repeatedly hardened Pharaoh's heart to make his glory known to Egypt and his name known throughout all the earth. The deliverance out of Egypt made God and his children famous. This one incident declared a God of might and covenant to the nations and distinguished Abraham's descendants for all eternity. Before this, Israel was an enslaved nation hidden within a free, prosperous, and powerful Egypt.

> **Fencing Fact**
>
> The art of fencing is about gaining control over your own actions. It is about self-discipline.

Later in the history of Israel, the nation was again faced with insurmountable odds—this time at the hands of the king of Assyria. He invited the children of Israel to enter into an unholy alliance with him and promised abundant bread and vines in a land of captivity. Listen to his threats, and notice how well his boasting positioned God to show himself strong on his people's behalf.

Beware lest Hezekiah mislead you by saying, "The LORD will
deliver us." Has any of the gods of the nations delivered his land
out of the hand of the king of Assyria?… Who among all the gods
of these lands have delivered their lands out of my hand, that the
LORD should deliver Jerusalem out of my hand? (Isaiah 36:18, 20)

How did King Hezekiah have his people answer this arrogant, ruthless conqueror?

They were silent and answered him not a word, for the king's
command was, "Do not answer him." (verse 21)

Just because the people were silent doesn't mean they weren't dis-
traught. After they left the presence of this bully king, they tore their
clothes in despair and sent messengers that brought these threats to the
attention of their nation's king. Hezekiah laid all of it before the Lord
and closed with this request:

So now, O LORD our God, save us from his hand, that *all* the
kingdoms of the earth may know that you alone are the LORD.
(Isaiah 37:20)

I love this. It shows that the battle is so much larger than any of us
have the capacity to realize. This wasn't a showdown between nations;
it was another revelation of the one true God. These nations never even
met on the battlefield, because God had another strategy in mind.

Behold, I will put a spirit in him, so that he shall hear a rumor
and return to his own land, and I will make him fall by the sword
in his own land. (Isaiah 37:7)

The very one who bragged about his reputation among the nations fell prey to the power of a rumor. I love this example, because often we are tempted to make battles personal by responding to rumors, but when we do, we lose even when we imagine we are winning.

> *Speech is silver; silence is golden.*
> —ANCIENT EGYPTIAN PROVERB

Remember, when God has your back, your future is golden.

Individual Struggles

What about when the battle *is* personal?

Actually I wonder how many times God was armed and ready to do battle on my behalf and I sabotaged his miraculous deliverance with my own mouth?

To be quite honest, this sword of silence may be the most difficult one for me to wield, yet I find an ever-increasing need for the protection of its blade. Remaining silent when threatened seems to conflict with a posture of protection, especially since silence is often the stance required when you are accused or belittled.

The book of Proverbs promises us, "Fire goes out without wood, and quarrels disappear when gossip stops" (26:20, NLT).

The challenge is remaining silent until the last piece of wood is utterly consumed and the wind of time blows away the ashes of the conflict.

Sometimes silence means walking away from conversations that put you at risk. Other times it means refusing to open your mouth when others cannot seem to close theirs. Weapons that are the mightiest are often the hardest to hold. Our tongue can be a weapon of extensive destruction or an agent of healing. I am not talking about the silent treatment. I know how to do that one well. I am talking about walking away without saying or doing anything when you want to do and say everything.

Recently John and I rediscovered the power of silence. Like everyone, we are not immune to gossip. People talk. Sometimes it is out of malice, and at other times they are just trying to sort through an issue. Such was the case when an unresolved matter that involved us was repeatedly brought before us. The topic inserted itself in the company of both friends and strangers. At first we were silent. Then we were cautious and even judicious with our words, but as the frequency and intensity of the gossip increased, it just felt wrong to be careful with our words when others were being so careless with theirs. Why shouldn't we tell our side of the story?

One day there was yet another incident. In my opinion it was the most unjust to date. I felt the proverbial line had been crossed, and I moved right into the realm of outspoken.

Can I be honest? At first, talking openly felt good! What a relief to finally speak my mind. Other people even seemed relieved to hear our side of the story. Believe me, that stage was short lived as I stumbled from being measured and careful in what I was saying to being utterly careless. It was as though a dam had been opened, and I was having an awful time getting the water back under control. It was spreading out and traveling in streams and rivulets to places I never intended it to go.

Now other people were wading in the miry river I'd created and were losing their shoes in my mud. The greater the mess became, the more I wanted to blame the other party for starting the mud slide. It wasn't long before I realized I was in knee deep. John and I had both said too much, and we were surrounded by muddy water.

We both came to this realization while we were in two different states. We called each other and prayed together over the phone. Repentant, we apologized and confessed our misdeeds as much as we could, but from that point forward *mum* was our new favorite word.

David's Sword of Silence

If there had been any doubt that we had made the right decision, the next day in Sunday service it was laid to rest. That day we had a guest speaker I'd not heard before. He began to share some brilliant insights about David and Saul—how David had navigated being misrepresented to Saul, then misrepresented by Saul, then chased by Saul, forgiven by Saul, only to be misrepresented yet again, then chased once again by Saul from cave to cave and hiding place to hiding place. David would prove his innocence and loyalty, only to be lied about and chased all over again.

I knew the story well and felt as though I had lived this scenario repeatedly.

The guest speaker didn't stop there. He went on to explain how David almost became what he'd been running from. Wearied by all the altercations, David hoped he'd found a haven by protecting Nabal's men and sheep. David sent some of his young men to ask if they could be part of the sheep-shearing festival. You have to wonder at this point if David truly just wanted to be included.

His request was not well received. Not only were they banned from the celebration, but David's character was questioned:

Nabal answered David's servants, "Who is David? Who is the son of Jesse? There are many servants these days who are breaking away from their masters...." So David's young men turned away and came back and told him all this. (1 Samuel 25:10, 12)

How would you feel? David was dishonored in front of his men, and his identity and birthright were undermined by the accusation that he was an upstart fugitive. When David heard this, he snapped, and his response was a bit overcharged!

> And David said to his men, "Every man strap on his sword!" And every man of them strapped on his sword. David also strapped on his sword. And about four hundred men went up after David, while two hundred remained with the baggage. (verse 13)

David had reached his limit. He'd had enough of accusations that he was a rebellious servant when he was faithfully serving God. He had not run away; he had been driven away. Nabal was about to incur the wrath of years of frustration. David was so discouraged he even questioned the rewards of godliness. Listen to him:

> *Now David had said, "Surely in vain have I guarded all that this fellow has in the wilderness, so that nothing was missed of all that belonged to him,* and he has returned me evil for good. God do so to the enemies of David and more also, if by morning I leave so much as one male of all who belong to him." (verses 21–22, emphasis added)

David morphed from a protector shepherd to a "let's kill them all" leader, which is easy to do when you forget your rewarder is God, not man. Because David was a leader, all his men followed suit and sided with their offended chief. Without hesitation or question they leaped onto the backs of their horses with their swords at their sides.

Which brings me to yet another point. Just because everyone follows your lead doesn't necessarily mean you're right. People follow leaders, and even though David was a great leader, he needed some wisdom, because he was at the tail end of a rough season.

How did David get to such a place?

It is possible that David allowed the words of a ridiculous man to blur his vision. For some reason this insult and insinuation threatened to knock him off course. After so many years of trusting God with the outcomes, David was on the path of taking things into his own hands.

If you are not careful, listening to what other people say about you may cause you to forget who you actually are.

No matter how many times David proved his innocence to Saul, it could never put him on the throne. The throne was no longer Saul's to give. The kingdom had been ripped from his hands. God was positioning David by refining him through rejection, the very test Saul had failed.

> Listening to what other people say about you may cause you to forget who you actually are.

We all have critics and detractors. I don't know of one sphere of life that escapes the opinion of others. The trick is choosing to allow those critiques to refine, *not* define, us!

David had not been anointed by Samuel to kill Saul and Nabal; he was anointed to rule Israel. He was on the verge of God's promise being fulfilled in his life, and he almost lost it—all because the foolish Nabal distracted him.

Here's a warning for you: fools will appear to detour you right before you arrive where God wants you. What do fools say? They question the existence and presence of God. They say things like "God is not for you" or "godliness has no benefit" and "God is not working on your behalf."

Slaughtering the men he'd once protected would have been an awful answer to Nabal's question "Who is David?"

And how many sheep-shearing parties do you think David and his men would have been invited to after this kind of outburst? I am guessing none. David would have allowed Nabal's foolish comment to define him.

Thank God for Abigail, a courageous woman with the sword of wisdom by her side. She fell before David, thus honoring all that her husband had dishonored. And then she intentionally reminded David of who and whose he was.

> For the LORD will certainly make my lord a sure house, because my lord is fighting the battles of the LORD, and evil shall not be found in you so long as you live. If men rise up to pursue you and to seek your life, the life of my lord shall be bound in the bundle of the living in the care of the LORD your God. And the lives of your enemies he shall sling out as from the hollow of a sling. And when the LORD has done to my lord according to all the good that he has spoken concerning you and has appointed you prince over Israel, my lord shall have no cause of grief or pangs of conscience for having shed blood without cause or for my lord working salvation himself. And when the LORD has dealt well with my lord, then remember your servant. (verses 28–31)

There are some key takeaways for all of us here:

1. God alone establishes houses.
2. When we live under the directive of God's Spirit, God protects us.
3. God knows how to settle matters with our enemies.
4. We should never use our position with God to protect ourselves.
5. We are not to take judgment or salvation matters into our hands; both of these belong to our God.

Thankfully, David was stopped by Abigail's words, and he remembered God's hand and promises over his life. It wasn't long before the widowed Abigail became David's bride and the rejected servant became king.

> *Silence is the element in which great things fashion*
> *themselves together; that at length they may emerge,*
> *full-formed and majestic, into the daylight of Life,*
> *which they are thenceforth to rule.*
>
> —THOMAS CARLYLE

A New Kind of Weapon

Lovely mothers, sisters, daughters, and friends, chances are someone has insulted you. Maybe your name has been paired with insinuating accusations. Is there an invitation that never finds its way to your door? Please believe me, I understand. But are you truly willing to allow an insult or oversight to derail or sabotage your destiny? You long to strike, but the sword you now hold that you thought was anointed is actually called vengeance, and it is not yours to wield. Resheath your sword and lay it down!

Are you upset because you are riding alongside someone else who has been maligned and dishonored? Dismount immediately, remind her of God's promises, and tell her to stand still and watch God, our rear guard, take over. My friend, God will establish your house and watch over you as you go forth. You don't have to figure out what needs to happen to those you perceive to be enemies. God has it all sorted out; rest in the knowledge that he alone is the righteous judge. It is time we move away from postures of self-protection. God fights for us as we fight on behalf of others.

Take up a different kind of weapon—a sword called *silence*. This sword stays in the scabbard. It is the very sword Jesus sheathed with such mastery. It is the weapon he refused to draw. Through silence he saved our lives by laying down his own. Imagine what remaining still was like, knowing the might of heaven was available at his raised voice or hand. Imagine being silent as the puny rulers of earth mocked their Creator. Imagine being falsely accused when he was the very personification of justice (see John 5:22). Jesus wasn't silent because he had no answer. Jesus was silent because he was their answer.

> Then the high priest stood up and said to Jesus, "Well, aren't you going to answer these charges? What do you have to say for yourself?" But Jesus remained silent. (Matthew 26:62–63, NLT)

Not a word, not a whisper, not a heavy sigh, head shake, or rolling of the eyes. Just silence…like a lamb. It wasn't that Jesus had nothing to say; it was that he chose to say nothing.

In the same way, there are times when we feel we have so much to say. We have been falsely accused, misunderstood, and even brought before others who are not really looking for the truth. Keep your counsel to yourself, and watch for God's answer. Miranda rights are read at arrests to protect the potentially guilty with this warning—"you have the right to remain silent"—so they do not incriminate themselves without legal counsel. Sometimes we all need to be reminded that remaining silent is our right.

> *Nonviolence is a powerful and just weapon,*
> *which cuts without wounding and ennobles*
> *the man who wields it. It is a sword that heals.*
> —MARTIN LUTHER KING JR.

If Jesus, the very Son of God, the only innocent One, exercised his right to remain silent when he refused to defend himself in the face of death, surely we can do the same as we face life. Jesus silently stepped in and took our place in the battle for us.

Even though he was innocent, our guilt had been laid upon him like a garment, and he wasn't willing to take it off.

All we like sheep have gone astray;
    we have turned—every one—to his own way;
and the LORD has laid on him
    the iniquity of us all.

He was oppressed, and he was afflicted,
    yet he opened not his mouth;
like a lamb that is led to the slaughter,
    and like a sheep that before its shearers is silent,
    so he opened not his mouth. (Isaiah 53:6–7)

The world turned away from the One who made a way. Actually, Jesus spoke the loudest in his silence. There was no need for words of earth to be voiced when the word of heaven stood before them, silent, as they condemned themselves so that through him all would be saved.

What battle needs to be answered through your silence? To gauge this, look at the areas of life where you find it difficult to be silent.

When he was reviled, he did not revile in return; when he suffered, he did not threaten, but continued entrusting himself to him who judges justly. (1 Peter 2:23)

Are you ready to stand still and watch? Trusting God in the face of threats, insults, and insinuations is a constant, continual, and, in some seasons, even a daily process. My sisters, we can do this. Because he has already gone before us and made a way.

● ● ●

Dear Heavenly Father,

I come to you in the name of Jesus. This day I choose to lay aside my right to speak my mind, and I exercise my right to be silent. Holy Spirit, grant me the wisdom to know when to be silent and when to speak. As I still my heart before you, speak to me. Put a watch over my mouth that I might not sin against you. Forgive me for the times I've chased rumors. I submit to your wisdom and will rule my soul by the counsel of your Word. I will no longer allow what others say about me to define me. You gave your life to defend me, and you alone are truth and justice. Forgive me for the times I sought my own counsel and willfully spoke my mind. Come into every battle that now threatens to overwhelm me. I will stop fanning the flames of human conflict. I trust you when the assaults of the enemy threaten to overwhelm me. I will stand my ground silent and assured that you already have won this battle. In Jesus's name, amen.

13

Sword of Forgiveness
and Restoration

*Sometimes by losing a battle
you find a new way to win the war.*

—Donald Trump

Envision a sword resting at the foot of a throne. The sword is yielded for a moment so that later it may be wielded for a greater purpose. Conquering kings demanded fealty from the very knights who had once opposed them. Each noble of the new realm appeared before the king and laid both sword and himself prostrate at his new lord's feet. At times the king would put his foot on the knight's neck. In this posture the knight took an oath of fealty to his new master before his sword was returned.

In this chapter we have an opportunity to weigh our motives. It is important to discover if we are fighting against someone or something or truly fighting on their behalf.

For example, you can be against abortion, but that doesn't necessarily mean you are pro-life. It is one thing to hold signs at an abortion clinic and quite another to open up your heart and home to an unwed mother or an unwanted child. You may be against murder but do not really want to do what it takes to preserve life.

These types of transitions in our motives happen when we realize we are devoted to a greater cause than our individual rights and opinions. Though we are entrusted with a sword of the Spirit, we are not armed to harm. We release captives and prisoners rather than terrify and bind them. There is always something bigger going on.

Just as the weapons of our warfare were not forged from the corruptible substances of our earth, we do not wage war according to the rules of the planet of our birth. Weapons should be used according to the laws of the realm of their origin, and ours come from a place where the "metal" is refined into the essence of true light and the edges of swords are flawlessly honed to at once cut and heal. Therefore, the motivation for raising these remarkable spiritual weapons should likewise be refined.

The book of Galatians gives an extensive list of human weapons and their motivations: sorcery, hatred or enmity, fits of rage or wrath, strife, dissensions and divisions, heresies, envy, and murder. All of these earthbound instruments and their objectives are linked to the Fall.

In contrast to the effect of these "dirty" weapons, the apostle Paul gives us a window into the reason behind our power:

> For even if I boast a little too much of our authority, which the Lord gave for building you up and not for destroying you, I will not be ashamed. (2 Corinthians 10:8)

We do not fight to tear down but to build up. The authority heaven lends to us on earth is to destroy evil by doing good. Just because I have walked with the sword of God's Word on my hip for more than three decades doesn't mean I have always worn it well. At times I've brandished the sword in anger and punctured what needed to be healed. At other times I left the sword in its sheath when I needed to draw it and sever the ties binding captives.

When my children were young, there was a long season when my sword lay beside my bed as though napping. During this time I turned the Bible's pages to read the psalms as I drifted off to sleep. Months passed as I carefully avoided using the sharp edges of my sword to penetrate my busy world.

On these pages I want to take you through a long-term personal fencing match that was filled with mishaps and finally triumph.

• • •

Shortly after I became a Christian, I knew God's hand was on me to minister to others. I began to prepare in earnest even though I had no idea what this ministry might look like. I read my Bible, went to church every time the doors opened, attended seminars, and served. In one of these many meetings, a visiting minister proclaimed with great conviction that if your entire family was not saved, then you had no business preaching the Word of God to others. His reasoning was that if your own life was not compelling enough to convince those closest to you of the truth of the gospel, why should anyone else listen to what you had to say. I've since learned that his impassioned words were somewhat less than accurate, but at the time I took them fully to heart.

Since my father was the furthest thing from being saved, I intensified my times of prayer. He was a classic example of all that defined *heathen* and *lost*. He smoked incessantly, drank excessively, and couldn't form a sentence without the use of cuss words. My understanding is that he repeatedly cheated on my mother and abandoned his children.

John and I were living in Dallas, and the first time Dad visited us, I dragged him to church. Throughout the service I chanced sidelong glances at my father in the hope that he would feel the full weight of his sin, the disapproval of his daughter, and the conviction of the Holy Spirit. I didn't want there to be any room for doubt when the pastor posed the closing question: "If you were to die tonight, where would you go?"

I assumed at a minimum that my father would bow his head in contemplation, but instead he stared right back at the minister as though to say defiantly, "I am headed straight to hell, and you can go there too!"

My father didn't so much as flinch during the salvation invitation. Desperate, I took his arm in an attempt to drag him to the altar. Disgusted, he shook off my hand. *Maybe he doesn't understand what is at risk.* To bring clarity, I leaned in and whispered, "Dad, Jesus is the only way. If you don't pray the prayer, you are going to hell."

This insight did not go over well! As I remember it, there was a string of profanity. Any door to his heart that I'd imagined was open had slammed shut and been bolted tight.

My dad was relieved when he returned to his carefree life in sunny Florida and left his Bible-thumping daughter behind in Texas.

Not one to be put off so easily, I contacted friends of a friend in Florida and gave them my father's phone number. My faith soared as I prayed that somehow these complete strangers would turn out to be the perfect laborers for my father.

When this attempt failed, I decided it was time to pull out the big guns.

I set aside an entire weekend to fast and pray for Dad's conversion. I would not relent. I paced and prayed, lay prostrate on the floor and cried, knelt by my bed with my Bible open and recited God's promises. It wasn't long before I found myself staring at the phone, willing it to ring. I couldn't wait to hear my father's voice as he shared how he'd been snatched from the hold of Satan.

The phone never rang, but I did hear the voice of my Father. My heavenly one whispered a question into my spirit: *Lisa, do you know I love your father more than you love your father?*

In all honesty at the time I found this revelation a bit shocking, so I remained quiet. The whisper continued, *I want him with me more than you want him with me. Lisa, give him to me... You can't save him.*

Then God reminded me of a promise in his Word: *Didn't I say, "Believe on the Lord Jesus Christ, and thou shalt be saved, and thy house"* [*Acts 16:31,* KJV]*? That is my promise to you for your father. Believe it and stop being weird. Just love him.*

I opened my Bible to Acts and highlighted the verse, thus placing all my hope in his Word.

> *Faith is the deliberate confidence in the character of God whose ways you may not understand at the time.*
> —OSWALD CHAMBERS

● ● ●

Not long thereafter I gave birth to our first son, Addison, and our family moved to Florida, to the same city where my father lived. Then, right before Alec was born, my father lost his job and moved a few hours away to the Florida coast. He hoped for a new beginning, but finding a new position was difficult for a man his age. My father, who had once built custom homes and country clubs, found himself working maintenance. He spiraled into a depression, and his drinking went from nightly to throughout the day. He no longer visited us, and the times we went to see him, he was drunk before noon. The visits frightened my children. They didn't understand why my dad slurred his words or why he ranted and raved and called their mother by the name of his ex-wife.

Then one December everything changed. The day after Christmas we walked around to the back entrance of the condominium my father shared with his girlfriend. We expected to find them seated on the back porch, but instead we found a note taped to the sliding glass door. In spidery letters it said, "Sorry, I made other plans."

The note was not addressed to anyone, and it had no signature. We had called and confirmed the visit once again right before we left our house and drove for several hours. Other plans? I stood there numb, holding the scrawled note in my hand. I could hear my children questioning me, "Where's Papa?"

Scanning the beach spread out before us, I imagined my father laughing at us in the distance. I didn't know what to say. John answered the boys as we ushered them all back into the van.

I was crushed and ashamed. I apologized repeatedly to John and my boys. Then I cried off and on all the way home. *John's parents would never dream of running away to a bar, especially when they know their children and grandchildren are coming to visit.*

Five hours is a long time to spend in a van, especially when the reason for the trip never happened and the mother cries all the way. The two boys that could reach me from their car seats patted me and offered their reassurance in a form of a question: "Okay? Mommy, it's okay."

I tried to put a brave face on, but I wasn't okay.

The next day John left for Sweden. After I got him on his flight, I came home, sent the boys outside, put on some worship music, and lay down on the floor to pray and ask God some questions: *Why didn't my father love me? Why didn't he want to be with my children? When will your promise come true?*

I wept into the carpet. Suddenly it dawned on me... *I was fatherless!* My father wasn't gone; he just couldn't be bothered! He didn't want anything to do with me. I lent voice to my thoughts and gave myself over in earnest to my tears, but just as I entered the weeping zone, I heard what I could only describe as God laughing. The sound was so incredibly out of place in this moment that I lifted my head and looked around. Then

I heard him whisper, "You are looking at this all wrong. What you see as rejection I see as adoption."

What?

"When you are completely abandoned by your natural father, you are utterly adopted by me. In a sense your father has renounced any claim he had to you and your children. Now nothing stands between us. You are all mine."

Seriously? Was I hearing this correctly?

"If John needs something, he can call his father. If you need something, come directly to me."

Okay, wow!

At the very moment I realized I was fatherless, I discovered I was adopted! I had such a sense that God had been excited to share this with me. I found myself laughing at the wonder of this revelation. I dried my tears, stood, and lifted my hands and life in worship. Only a true, good Father would care for me like this!

From that moment forward I did not look for anything from my father. He owed me nothing—not visits, approval, love, gifts, or even kind words.

Shortly after this realization our family moved from Florida to Colorado, and visits with my father became few and far between. Because of Dad's heavy drinking, I'd no longer felt safe when I went to see him. Before we finally left the state, I invited my father to come and stay in our home and say good-bye to us. He flatly refused. So I left Florida, still holding on to the promise of God that my father would be saved.

• • •

The next time my brother, Joey, and I visited our father, he wasn't sure who I was. The many years of alcohol abuse had distorted his perceptions. For the majority of our visit, he imagined I was an ex-girlfriend or an ex-wife. When he finally realized I was his daughter, he looked me up and down and thanked me for losing weight. Apparently, he'd been appalled by how chubby I had appeared on the last Christmas card. These same tactics would have sent me into an eating disorder when I was fifteen.

I tried to show him the pictures of my boys and share stories from their lives, but he wouldn't hear of it. My brother took a video of him so I could take something home to my boys. But when he was being recorded, he cursed and flipped off the camera. I left feeling like a dirty disappointment.

As I flew home, I heard God whisper the promises of Psalm 45 again over my life:

> Hear, O daughter, and consider, and incline your ear:
>   forget your people and your father's house,
>   and the king will desire your beauty.
> Since he is your lord, bow to him. (verses 10–11)

I knew I would never again feel pressured to bow to the imagery my broken father laid before me. I was the desire of my King.

● ● ●

The years moved on, and my father's dementia progressed to the place where his girlfriend had no choice but to put him in a high-security facility.

In December 2009 I visited him one last time. I brought along my firstborn son, Addison, his lovely wife, Julianna, and their newborn son, Asher. I wanted my father to see his first great-grandchild. When we arrived at Dad's care facility, I spread out pictures on the table before him, hoping he would make the connections of who we were. One photo was of Dad and Addison when Addison was a year old. I pointed to the young man who now towered over my father and explained that he was my son—his grandson. My father nodded as he gently handled the pictures in an attempt to take it all in.

Then it happened. I could almost see the fibers of Dad's memories weaving together the fabric of his family. He lifted his head and looked at me, Juli, Asher, and Addison, each in turn. Suddenly I knew he understood. He bobbed his head gently and pointed knowingly from the picture in his hand to Addison. As he recognized us, I could once again see beyond his frail frame to the man he had been. He was present with us, but I had no idea for how long.

I lifted a silent prayer: *Heavenly Father, what should I say?*

The response was shocking and immediate: *Tell him he was a good dad.*

What? Stunned, I countered, *That's a lie! I am not going to lie to him... especially not now! He was not a good father.*

I heard a firm assurance: *He was as good as he knew how to be.*

In disbelief I argued, *He could have learned how to be better.* My mind traveled back to the neighbors he could have befriended and the books he could have read. As far as I could remember, he'd never even tried!

My rebuttal was met with silence. Over the decades I've learned that God doesn't argue. I can argue for as long as I want, but in the end what he last said is what stands as his final answer. It was time I used the sword of restoration to heal.

I drew a deep breath, reached over, and took my father's hands in mine. I lifted them between us to draw his attention, looked him in the eyes, and repeated what I had heard: "Dad, you were a good dad."

My father was stunned. It was as though a tremor passed through his entire body, and his eyes brimmed with tears. He kissed the back of my hands and with great effort formed these two words: "Thank...you."

> **Fencing Fact**
>
> Two skillful fencers acting together fight more with their heads than with their hands.

With those words everything changed. The stifled atmosphere of the nursing home felt lighter, and I realized my father's heart had just opened. Julianna began to cry, and Addison moved quickly to stand behind the chair in which my father was seated. We all began to pray over my father according to the promise in Acts that God had given me so long ago. We thanked God for my father's salvation and canceled any debts he might feel he owed, according to John 20:23:

> If you forgive the sins of any, they are forgiven them; if you with-
> hold forgiveness from any, it is withheld.

The entire time we prayed, my father squeezed my hands in affirmation and continued to rain kisses on the back of my hands. It was a holy moment of love and forgiveness. His gestures were pure and innocent, like a child's. There was no hint of the lewdness I'd experienced on my past visits.

When it was over, Dad was visibly tired. While Julianna stayed behind with Asher, Addison and I accompanied him back to his sparsely furnished bedroom and tucked him into bed. Before leaving I checked with his nurse to confirm that my contact information was correct. As I filled out a slip of paper for her to add to his file, my father wandered out of his room. I called to him, but he walked right past us as though we were complete strangers and sat down with a group of women who were watching a rerun of *The Lawrence Welk Show.* Something had happened in our time together, but Dad was gone again.

•   •   •

A year passed, and Christmas 2010 came. I remember feeling troubled whenever I thought about my father. I would wake in the middle of the night and wonder if he was dying. I shared my concerns with my mother, who assured me that my aunt and uncle had just visited him and that he was fine. But for some reason I couldn't shake a feeling of foreboding. I told Joey I thought it was important that he go to see Dad as soon as possible.

As I prepared dinner on New Year's Eve, I watched a news commentator share about the passing of her father and how much she missed him. Tears began to trace my cheeks. I froze. Why was I crying? I did not know this woman or her father. I heard the Spirit whisper, *You are crying because this is the year you will say good-bye to your father.*

January 6 found me in Canada on a ministry trip. I woke up excessively early and troubled in my hotel room. It was 3:00 a.m., and no matter how hard I tried, I could not get back to sleep. Later that morning I was taping five television shows and a series of teachings that required mental clarity. I prayed, read, and listened to music—but to no avail.

I felt shaky and unsettled all morning, and with each passing hour my unease increased.

When the tapings were over and I was headed to the airport, I turned on my cell phone and saw that I had missed quite a few calls. The first voice message was from my youngest son at home. He had lost his retainer and needed me to call the orthodontist to authorize a replacement. I worked my way through the messages until only one was left. I was in a rush to catch my flight and go through customs, so I decided I would listen to the last message as I walked to my gate.

After gathering my carry-on items, I pushed Play. A woman's voice said, "As you know, your father is dying. If you want to say good-bye to him, you will have to come today."

Before the message ended, I dialed her number. My mind was reeling. *How would I have known this? No one had told me my father was dying.* Mercifully, I was able to reach the woman who was in her car on her way to my father's hospice room. I explained that I was in Canada, ready to board a flight to Denver. She promised to call me back as soon as she was at my father's side.

Next I tried to reach my brother, but he was in meetings. I called John and one of my friends. My world was spinning. I checked for direct flights to Orlando, but none was available.

Out of time, I boarded my flight for Denver, and while other passengers walked by, I waited for her call. Just before the attendants closed the door and ordered all phones to be switched off, she called. She explained that Dad was not well and offered to put her phone up to his ear. I turned my face away from an aisle filled with people and into the privacy of the window's oval.

"Dad, this is Lisa." My voice sounded small and shaky, but I went on. "I love you. Remember how you took me fishing and taught me to dive and swim? I am coming tomorrow, but if you can't hold your breath any longer under water, you can go."

I paused, wondering what more to say. The woman came on the phone again. I asked her if she had seen any sign that Dad had heard me. She explained that she couldn't see any evidence of a response, but she believed that on some level he had heard me. I realized that it was past time to turn off my phone, so I said good-bye.

I read for the entire three-and-a-half-hour trip. To be honest, I don't remember what book it was. As soon as I landed, I tried to reach my brother. I dialed his number again and again until I was able to reach him and share what was going on.

Joey began to make plans to travel from California to Florida. I spoke with the airlines on the phone as I traveled home through the dark, cold night of a Colorado winter. I planned to leave on the seven o'clock flight the next morning. As soon as I got home, I gathered my boys and shared the news with them. As they listened, I realized my father was a complete stranger to them. I told them how sorry I was to be leaving again when I had just returned home and their father was out of town.

At that moment both my home and cell phone rang. On one line was my married son; the second caller was my brother. He told me our father was gone. That was it. There would be no funeral, because Dad had arranged for his body to be cremated. We'd never see him again. I spoke again with my dad's social worker and cried as I told her that he was gone.

I went to bed that night, sad, wrapped in blankets and prayer: "God, you're faithful."

I slept deeply and woke surprisingly rested.

• • •

I was home for another week before my travel schedule kicked in. Over the months of January, February, March, and April, I spoke to crowds ranging from hundreds to thousands, and each evening I declared the faithfulness of God. I tried not to think about my father. He was out of my hands. Then in May 2011, I met up with the faithfulness of God.

I was speaking at a women's conference in Jacksonville, Florida. In my first session I noticed an adorable young woman with spiky red hair. For some reason, amid a crowd of more than a thousand, she was the one person I remembered. Then I noticed her again at an afternoon breakout session.

That evening as I was about to leave for my next session, I saw this cute red-haired woman again in my hotel lobby and felt compelled to introduce myself. I approached her, but before I could say anything, she introduced herself.

"Lisa, I am April. We spoke on the phone."

My mind searched for any memories of speaking to someone named

April from Jacksonville. She noticed I had drawn a blank and began to fill in the spaces for me.

"I am the one who called you the day your father died."

I shook my head, trying to figure out the five-to-six-hour-drive distance between my father's nursing home and Jacksonville. *Why was April here?*

"I drove up with some of my friends to be at this conference when I heard you'd be here." I was speechless.

April continued, "I was your father's social worker for the last five years. He was an awful patient. He was kicked out of the first facility he was placed in. He ran away, he was violent, he stole a car, and he was beat up by the police. But for the last year, he was an angel."

I was still stunned, looking at her blankly.

"He kissed my hand whenever I saw him," she went on to say.

My mind reeled as I tried to take it all in. Had she just said my dad had been an angel the last year of his life?

"April, I came to see him a year before he died."

"I know. I saw your name in his file. I have read your books, but before your visit I didn't make the connection that he was your father. I prayed for him for years and wanted to be certain you had a chance to tell him good-bye."

God is faithful. Not only did he surround my father with prayer when I was not with him, but I have every reason to believe my father received more than just my forgiveness when we prayed. I believe somehow in that moment he received heaven's forgiveness as well. My father had gone overnight from difficult to compliant, from angry and embittered to childlike and loving. It would appear that in the last year of his life he had borne the fruit of repentance. There is so much I will never know or understand until I am in eternity, but I feel certain I will see my father there.

Forgiveness is the remission of sins. For it is by this that what
has been lost, and was found, is saved from being lost again.
—AUGUSTINE

I often wonder if, on the night we visited him, my father remembered all that he had lost. I wonder if the innocence of his great-grandson, Asher, awoke hope of a legacy he thought all but gone. I wonder if he looked at the strength and maturity of Addison and the beauty and grace of Juli and saw young love. I wonder if I represented the family he'd lost. That night we found him in a place where he could no longer run away. We saw the pain he had tried to numb for years with alcohol and just loved him.

What's Your Story?

Now, Lovely One, how about you? I don't know your story, but I can tell you that God is faithful. Are there any daggers of disappointment or bitterness that might threaten to misdirect a sword in your hand? The truth is, I still judged my father until the moment I spoke the words God gave me. When I released him, I was likewise released. Our King has a way of healing both parties through the actions of one.

Deep wounds that remain unhealed can cause us to lash out and injure the very ones heaven longs to heal. The King has conquered your heart; now he wants to use your life for his purpose of restoration.

There is no revenge so complete as forgiveness.
—JOSH BILLINGS

Let's lay any sword of rejection and disappointment at our Father's feet and allow him to remake it into adoption, restoration, and divine appointments. How might God want to use you as an agent of restoration? Where can the King send you to speak the words others need to hear in order to receive his healing and life? Are you willing to speak his counsel rather than the words you have rehearsed? Are you willing to bless someone who has hurt you? I am not asking you to repeat my words, but I am asking you to speak our Father's words into situations and individuals that are crying out to be restored.

• • •

Dear Heavenly Father,

I lay my life before you as an act of fealty. I am tired of fighting from a position of disappointment. You are faithful to your word, and you love and do all things well. I surrender all that I have carried in my own strength. I give you the timing and ask that you give me your wisdom and words. I choose to give you all my loyalty and devotion. Raise me up armed to heal, rather than harm, in Jesus's name. Amen.

• • •

As we transition into our last section, I realize there is not room enough to outline each and every sword you can carry, for swords are highly personalized weapons. In the next section I hope to challenge you never again to leave home unarmed.

PART FOUR

COMMISSIONED

14

Cross Carry

We must wake ourselves up! Or somebody
else will take our place, and bear our cross,
and thereby rob us of our crown.

—William Booth

You and I possess both a cross and a crown. For the most part the cross we carry is invisible. We see its effect but not its form. Likewise, in Christ we have been given an invisible crown.

> What is man, that you are mindful of him,
>   or the son of man, that you care for him?
> You made him for a little while lower than the angels;
>   you have crowned him with glory and honor,
>   putting everything in subjection under his feet.
>   (Hebrews 2:6–8)

On the earth the crown represents our position of authority. As ambassadors of heaven, we are backed by the power of that realm.

Learn to know Christ and him crucified. Learn
to sing to him, and say, "Lord Jesus, you are my

righteousness, I am your sin. You have taken
upon yourself what is mine and given me what is
yours. You have become what you were not so that
I might become what I was not."

—Martin Luther

We wear the crown, and we carry the cross. Jesus bore our cross so we could wear his crown. He became like us. Isn't it time we became like him?

> Then Jesus told his disciples, "If anyone would come after me, let him deny himself and take up his cross and follow me."
> (Matthew 16:24)

How do we fulfill this highly personalized directive?

There are three elements in this instruction: deny yourself, lift the cross, and follow Jesus. My selfish ways are different from yours, just as the cross I take up is unique to my journey. I do not carry your cross, nor do you carry mine.

In order to learn how to carry our cross, we must first answer some questions concerning the cross. What exactly is Jesus asking us to carry? Where do we find our cross? Is it a burden we drag through the course of our lives? Or does the cross stand for something vastly more mysterious than any wooden beams could represent? The cross has a beauty so great that no necklace or pendant could ever compare. I truly believe the cross captures all that the work of salvation has placed in our hands.

The cross is far from an ornament to wear; it is an order to carry out. In this closing chapter I want to share what it looks like to carry your cross like a hero.

A Conversation About the Cross

It was almost two o'clock in the morning on the eve of Easter. I was just drifting off to sleep when the Holy Spirit began to question me about the cross.

"Lisa, what does it mean to carry your cross?"

Sleepily I answered, "To deny myself."

I heard distinctly, "No, denying yourself is only the first step."

I volunteered hesitatingly, "To lay down my will?"

"Denying yourself is laying down your will. What does it mean to carry your cross?"

In that moment I realized I probably didn't have the answer, but that didn't stop the questions.

"How do you know when you are carrying your cross or when you've left it at home?"

"How much does your cross weigh, Lisa?"

"Where do you keep your cross?"

Images of my messy closet, the garage, and a spot by the front door flew through my head. Bleary-eyed, I sat up in bed and whispered aloud, "I don't know…"

With my admission the barrage of questions ceased. To be honest, I have written on the cross in one capacity or another in each of my books, and now it seemed I couldn't even locate mine, let alone describe it!

I love how the very moment we admit our need, God is there to meet it. As soon as I acknowledged my ignorance, the answers began to be revealed. I heard, "Go get the list you made earlier today."

As I mentioned in chapter 5, I had polled my social media outlets and gathered more than a few single-word descriptions of the Cross. What I didn't tell you was that I had tallied more than five hundred responses by hand on a discarded envelope. I went into John's office, found the scrap of paper, and brought it back to bed with me. I transferred the scribbled list onto my iPad. Here are some of the words I received, presented graphically:

I had taken the poll, searching for one particular answer that I was not given, but I will add it here: *weapon.* As I reviewed the list of words that so many were kind enough to volunteer, I heard the Holy Spirit whisper, "Behold the Cross. All of these words and more represent the Cross. Carry these with you into your everyday world."

My eyes retraced the list in my trembling hand. It was true! *The Cross provides all that it won, just as Jesus provides all that he is!* Through the Cross, Christ purchased us love, forgiveness, freedom, and redemption. It was time I carried all I had experienced to others. Each of these words captured some of the elemental essences of the Cross that needed to be expressed to the lost world. (And even to quite a few churches.) Paul described his cross-carry this way:

> We carry this precious Message [of the Cross] around in the un-adorned clay pots of our ordinary lives. (2 Corinthians 4:7, MSG)

The cross I carry is all that he has done for me, just as the cross you carry is your gospel, or witness, of what he has done for you. But it doesn't stop there. We are containers that pour out heaven's precious gifts. We do not filter the gospel; we just carry it. In this way the extraordinary is transferred within the confines of our daily ordinary. Each day I take the hope, love, and forgiveness of the Cross with me to the grocery store, on the plane, and to the office. I carry it everywhere my life takes me. These are the places where I offer the power and wonder of the Cross.

Listen as Paul describes this dynamic of carrying the Cross to the new believers in Rome:

> So here's what I want you to do, God helping you: Take your everyday, ordinary life—your sleeping, eating, going-to-work, and walking-around life—and place it before God as an offering. *Embracing what God does for you is the best thing you can do for him.* Don't become so well-adjusted to your culture that you fit into it without even thinking. Instead, *fix your attention on God.* You'll be changed from the inside out. Readily recognize what he wants from you, and quickly respond to it. (Romans 12:1–2, MSG, emphasis added)

Jesus didn't hold formal crusades, conferences, or even weekly services. Yet every waking moment of his life was a message. (There is nothing wrong with these, but they are rarely part of our everyday lives.) Jesus carried God with him every day, everywhere he went, and he is asking you to do the same. Embracing all of what God has done for you and reflecting this new life to others can be likened to taking up the cross. As we lay hold of this truth, we carry ourselves and see our world differently. What if each day we prayed, "Heavenly Father, may everything that the crucifixion of your Son provided gain full expression in and through my life today. I choose to deny sin and my former limitations as I magnify your work and follow you"?

Fencing Fact

Fence when you're tired, when you're sick, when it's too hot, when it's too cold, when it's raining, when you hate fencing.

Our world would see Jesus lifted up.

When this exchange happens, our gaze shifts. Instead of looking at ourselves, we become attentive to the life of Jesus. By reading our Bible, we learn the way he moved through his days. What we were freely given, we freely give.

Our Cross-Carry

Let's walk through this together. Do we agree that the Cross was God's ultimate display of his unconditional love for us? Do you have any doubt that untold millions still wait for us to carry the expression of this unconditional love to them? How do we do this? We follow his example.

Jesus *loved* people by speaking truth, feeding the hungry, casting out demons, healing the sick, confronting religion, and raising the dead.

> And he went throughout all Galilee, *teaching* in their synagogues
> and *proclaiming the gospel of the kingdom* and *healing every disease*

and every affliction among the people. (Matthew 4:23, emphasis added)

Follow him.

What about forgiveness? Is there less need for forgiveness today, or are far too many trapped in guilt and shame? Carry the cross of forgiveness to them by freely forgiving and sharing the good news that they have been freely forgiven.

Jesus showed people they were *forgiven* by speaking truth, feeding the hungry, casting out demons, healing the sick, confronting religion, and raising the dead.

> "Take heart, my son; your sins are forgiven." And behold, some of the scribes said to themselves, "This man is blaspheming." But Jesus, knowing their thoughts, said, "Why do you think evil in your hearts? For which is easier, to say, 'Your sins are forgiven,' or to say, 'Rise and walk'? *But that you may know that the Son of Man has authority on earth to forgive sins"*—he then said to the paralytic—*"Rise, pick up your bed and go home."* And he rose and went home. When the crowds saw it, they were afraid, and they *glorified God, who had given such authority to men.* (Matthew 9:2–8, emphasis added)

Follow him.

He did this so we would know that the authority to heal and forgive had been given to us. He did this miracle as the Son of Man! How much more should we do this as daughters of God?

Then there are the issues of freedom. Has there ever been a generation so ensnared by lust, greed, idolatry, and depravity? And there are those who have literally been enslaved for labor or trafficked for sex. Carry the cross of freedom to them. You may wonder, *How?* Jesus showed people they were *free* by speaking truth, feeding the hungry, casting out demons, healing the sick, confronting religion, and raising the dead.

> *God anointed Jesus of Nazareth with the Holy Spirit and with power.*
> *He went about doing good and healing all who were oppressed by the*
> *devil, for God was with him.* (Acts 10:38, emphasis added)

Follow him.

Jesus did good and healed all who were oppressed by the devil because God was with him! There is no reason to choose between social justice and the supernatural. Jesus did both. Let's remove our name from the equation, call him Immanuel—"God with us"—and do the same.

There is a glaring need for redemption on every front of the human condition. The word *redemption* has a massive reach, and by definition it includes salvation, exchange, deliverance, rescue, refurbishment, restoration, and recovery. Has the need for all of these in any way diminished? Express the cross of that purchased redemption to others by your daily life.

Again, Jesus showed people they were *redeemed* by speaking truth, feeding the hungry, casting out demons, healing the sick, confronting religion, and raising the dead.

> Let the redeemed of the LORD say so,
>   whom he has redeemed from trouble. (Psalm 107:2)

After this admonition, Psalm 107 records a list of circumstances that got God's people into trouble. It will encourage you to know you are not alone, so you should read it. It was just too long to put on these pages! Know this, whether you've messed up or found yourself in a mess due to no fault of your own, *God redeems*. Regardless of how we got into a place of trouble, he leads us out and into his place of goodness. He alone has the power to save, and we who've been redeemed should say so! It is another way we carry our cross.

> For you will not abandon my soul to Sheol,
>> or let your holy one see corruption.
>
> You make known to me the path of life;
>> in your presence there is fullness of joy;
>> at your right hand are pleasures forevermore. (Psalm 16:10–11)

The words are David's, but the promise was first Christ's and is now ours.

Follow him.

No matter where you are right now, this is the promise of the redeemed. This is the power of the Cross. What other emblem has the power to proclaim the gospel of the kingdom better? Did Christ's sacrifice on the cross heal your life, body, and relationships? Do you believe it still has the power to heal every disease and affliction? We know that Jesus is the same yesterday, today, and forever. Can't the same be said of the Cross? Jesus again charged his disciples to follow his example after his resurrection.

> And when they saw him they worshiped him, but some doubted. And Jesus came and said to them, "All authority in heaven and on earth has been given to me. Go therefore and make disciples of all

nations, baptizing them in the name of the Father and of the Son and of the Holy Spirit, teaching them to observe all that I have commanded you. And behold, I am with you always, to the end of the age." (Matthew 28:17–20)

If he is with us and he is the same, then he is willing to display on earth all that the Cross has purchased.

Afterward he appeared to the eleven themselves as they were reclining at table, and he rebuked them for their unbelief and hardness of heart, because they had not believed those who saw him after he had risen. And he said to them, "Go into all the world and proclaim the gospel to the whole creation. Whoever believes and is baptized will be saved, but whoever does not believe will be condemned. And these signs will accompany those who believe: in my name they will cast out demons; they will speak in new tongues; they will pick up serpents with their hands; and if they drink any deadly poison, it will not hurt them; they will lay their hands on the sick, and they will recover." (Mark 16:14–18)

Jesus first had to address a few things before all his disciples could follow him and see the signs and wonders: doubt, unbelief, and hard hearts. We don't need to chase after demons, but if you follow Jesus long enough, you will probably encounter them. Don't strike up a conversation with them! Use the sword of God's Word to silence them, and then cast them out in Jesus's name.

Speak heaven's truth in every language you can.

Snake handling and intentionally drinking poison are just stupid. Since Jesus would not throw himself off a cliff, he surely was not inviting his disciples to play with poisonous snakes and drink deadly elixirs. The takeaway here is the promise of protection. He promised that as we touched the sick, recovery would happen. The sick should no longer be considered the unclean whom we are afraid to come into contact with. Jesus touched and was touched by the unclean, and the contact healed them. You may say, "Well, that was Jesus." I remember reading that when Mother Teresa chose to come into contact with the lepers, the treatment that stopped the spread of this highly infectious disease was discovered.[10]

> Now many signs and wonders were regularly done among the
> people by the hands of the apostles. And they were all together
> in Solomon's Portico.... And every day, in the temple and from
> house to house, they did not cease teaching and preaching that
> the Christ is Jesus. (Acts 5:12, 42)

Signs and wonders and teaching and preaching should be everyday events. At this point I must confess…I want the supernatural to be more natural and the greatness of his name declared every day. So to this end I am going to speak his name and follow Jesus's lead. If the early church took the message of the Cross everywhere they went, and hearts were encouraged, the sick were healed, and the oppressed were set free, why shouldn't the same be true of us?

Are you looking for a sign that Jesus still wants to do wonders? The Cross is our sign, and you are his wonder!

I believe we will see signs and wonders to the degree that we preach the Cross of Christ and live the Word of God. A minimalistic gospel produces minimal results. Preaching only half of the benefits of the Cross will produce only half of the Cross's benefits. Derivatives cannot be expected to produce what an original will at full strength.

My speech and my preaching was not with enticing words of
man's wisdom, but in demonstration of the Spirit and of power:
That your faith should not stand in the wisdom of men, but in
the power of God. (1 Corinthians 2:4–5, KJV)

Preaching a powerless gospel produces minimal power. The blood of
Jesus made a way for us to approach the throne with boldness so that we
can find all the power of heaven we need.

Let us hold fast the confession of our hope without wavering, for
he who promised is faithful. And let us consider how to stir up one
another to love and good works, not neglecting to meet together,
as is the habit of some, but encouraging one another, and all the
more as you see the Day drawing near. (Hebrews 10:23–25)

Living Swords

I have written all this in the hope that it will stir you. For far too long
we have scratched ears and tickled human fancy with the sleight of our
hands. It is time we extend our reach by becoming his sword.

Come home, hope-filled prisoners!
	This very day I'm declaring a double bonus—
	everything you lost returned twice-over!
Judah is now my weapon, the bow I'll pull,
	setting Ephraim as an arrow to the string.
I'll wake up your sons, O Zion,
	to counter your sons, O Greece.
From now on
	people are my swords. (Zechariah 9:12–13, MSG, emphasis added)

Just as Jesus was the Word of the Father made flesh, our lives are to become the Word of Jesus made flesh. Because the Word of God is the sword of the Spirit and Jesus was the Word made flesh, as his body we, too, become living swords. "He makes his messengers winds, his ministers a flaming fire" (Psalm 104:4). We are flaming swords who proclaim he is the way.

> Just as Jesus was the Word of the Father made flesh, our lives are to become the Word of Jesus made flesh.

His Spirit is the wind that propels us, and his message is the fire shut up in our bones. All that he has done for us and all that he yet longs to do should not be restrained by our self-doubt and religious traditions. The Cross left nothing undone. Why have we done so little?

The Cross has positioned you to be a hero. You should carry it as one with hope in your heart, faith for the impossible, and love for all humanity. The disciples didn't have the length of days or even the room to record all the things Jesus did.

> Now there are also many other things that Jesus did. Were every one of them to be written, I suppose that the world itself could not contain the books that would be written. (John 21:25)

This means that the wonder of Jesus is immeasurable. Yet I believe each of us has been chosen as a living expression of his wonder. As we become one with him, as he is one with the Father, then the world will glimpse his bride in full stature, and many will be won.

Daughter of God, turn from your reflection, deny its limitations, and reflect him. Daily remind yourself of his goodness, redemption, and mercy. Listen to the Holy Spirit as you carry all that the Cross provided to those who wait in hope. Read and recite the verses of your King until they overflow into every aspect of your life as you follow him. Lovely One, no longer think of yourself as targeted, because you were first chosen to be a sword lifted in his hand. Live like a hero, and you will strike a sure blow to the enemy, and captives will be set free.

> *Men have said that the cross of Christ was not a heroic thing, but I want to tell you that the cross of Jesus Christ has put more heroism in the souls of men than any other event in human history.*
> —JOHN G. LAKE

NOTES

1. Mara Hvistendahl, *Unnatural Selection* (Philadelphia, PA: Perseus, 2011), 6.

2. C. S. Lewis, *The Screwtape Letters* (New York: HarperCollins, 1942), 200.

3. Lewis, *The Screwtape Letters,* 4.

4. Nick Evangelista, *The Art and Science of Fencing* (Lincolnwood, IL: Masters Press, 1996), 126–27.

5. Evangelista, *The Art and Science of Fencing,* 126.

6. "Moment (physics)," http://en.wikipedia.org/wiki/Moment _%28physics%29.

7. "Trafficking in Persons Report," June 2008, www.state.gov /documents/organization/105501.pdf, 9.

8. Pete Brookshaw, "The Greatest Challenges Facing the Salvation Army Today," www.petebrookshaw.com/2012/07 /greatest-challenges-facing-salvation.html, July 1, 2012.

9. "Flame-bladed sword," http://en.wikipedia.org/wiki /Flame-bladed_sword.

10. David Van Biema, *Mother Teresa: The Life and Works of a Modern Saint* (New York: Time Books, 2010), 37.

OTHER TITLES
BY LISA BEVERE

LIONESS ARISING

NURTURE

FIGHT LIKE A GIRL

KISSED THE GIRLS AND MADE THEM CRY

BE ANGRY BUT DON'T BLOW IT!

OUT OF CONTROL AND LOVING IT!

THE TRUE MEASURE OF A WOMAN

YOU ARE NOT WHAT YOU WEIGH

Messenger International.
teach reach rescue

UNITED STATES

PO BOX 888
PALMER LAKE, CO 80133

TOLL FREE: 800-648-1477
PHONE: 719-487-3000
FAX: 719-487-3300

UNITED KINGDOM

PO BOX 1066
HEMEL HEMPSTEAD
HERTFORDSHIRE, HP2 7GQ
UNITED KINGDOM

FREEPHONE: 0800 9808 933
OUTSIDE UK:
PHONE: +44 1442 288 531

AUSTRALIA

PO BOX 6444
ROUSE HILL TOWN CENTRE
ROUSE HILL, NSW 2155

PHONE: 1-300-650-577
FAX: 1-300-650-578
OUTSIDE AUSTRALIA:
PHONE: +61 2 9679 4900
FAX: +61 2 9679 1588

MESSENGERINTERNATIONAL.ORG

 @LISABEVERE